Heinemann **Scottish** History

The Age of Revolutions
1700-1900

Elizabeth Trueland

Series editor: Jim McGonigle

Heinemann

Heinemann Educational Publishers
Halley Court, Jordan Hill, Oxford, OX2 8EJ
a division of Reed Educational & Professional Publishing Ltd

Heinemann is a registered trademark of Reed Educational & Professional Publishing Ltd

OXFORD MELBOURNE AUCKLAND

JOHANNESBURG BLANTYRE GABORONE

IBADAN PORTSMOUTH NH (USA) CHICAGO

© Elizabeth Trueland 2002

First published 2002

ISBN 0 435 32092 0
04 03 02
10 9 8 7 6 5 4 3 2 1

Designed and typeset by Ken Vail Graphic Design, Cambridge

Illustrated by SGA (Ross Watton)

Printed and bound in the United Kingdom by Bath Colourbooks

Picture research by Virginia Stroud-Lewis

Photographic acknowledgements
The author and publisher would like to thank the following for permission to reproduce photographs:
Bridgeman Art Library/Musee de la Ville: 48A; British Museum: 21B; Glasgow Museums: 25C, 41E; Hulton Archive: 39C; Hulton-Deutsch Collection: 31B, 59A, 62D; Mary Evans Picture Library: 31A; Mitchell Library, State Library of New South Wales: 55I; National Gallery of Scotland: 5C, 11B, 13A, 64H; National Library of Scotland: 5B, 36F, 41F, 42A, 53D; National Trust for Scotland/Allan Forbes: 28C; Natural History Museum: 55J; Royal Collection © HM Queen Elizabeth II/A.C. Cooper: 18G; Royal Commission on the Ancient and Historical Monuments of Scotland: 35E; Scottish National Portrait Gallery: 9C; Tate Picture Library: 22C; Trustees of the National Museums of Scotland: 54E, 58F

Cover photograph: © Sotheby's Picture Library. The painting is 'A Terminus in the West' by Forbes, 1925.

Written acknowledgements
The authors and publisher gratefully acknowledge the following publications from which written sources in the book are drawn. In some sources the wording or sentence structure has been simplified.

L. Colley, *Britons Forging the Nation 1707–1837* (Pimlico, 1992): 23B
T. Devine, *The Scottish Nation 1700–2000* (Allen Lane, 1999): 4A, 8A, 14B, 45D, 54G, 62C
B. Lenman, *The Jacobite Risings in Britain, 1689–1746* (Methuen, 1980): 9B, 62B
M. Lynch, *Scotland: A New History* (Pimlico, 1992): 29E, 64F
M. McLeod, *Leaving Scotland* (National Museums of Scotland, 1996): 54H
J. Patrick, *Scotland: The Age of Achievement* (John Murray, 1985): 28D
T.C. Smout, *A History of the Scottish People* (Fontana, 1972): 6F
T.C. Smout, *A Century of the Scottish People* (Collins, 1986): 61A

Contents

Living in Scotland around 1700

— After the Act of Union – what did the Scots think?

In 1707 Scotland and England signed the Act of Union. This meant that Scotland no longer had its own parliament and that, from then on, Scotland would have 45 members of parliament (MPs) in the British Parliament in London. In exchange, the Scots were allowed to trade freely with England, as well as with the growing number of England's colonies overseas. This had not been allowed before. As a result, produce such as linen, grain and cattle could be sold in England or in England's colonies. England was a much wealthier country than Scotland before the Union and many of those who signed the Act of Union believed that it would bring increased prosperity to Scotland.

There were many others, though, who regretted Scotland's loss of independence and feared that the Union had been drawn up to meet the needs of the English and not the Scots. In particular, many Scots did not like the fact that it would take time to see the benefits of the Union. Also, the new taxes imposed by the London government, and the tax collectors who made sure that these taxes were paid, were very unpopular. The new parliament also decided that landowners could appoint church ministers, which undermined the independence of the Church of Scotland.

— What was it like to live in Scotland around 1700?

Historians use many different types of evidence to try to answer questions like this. Evidence can be primary – of the time; or secondary – opinions and reconstructions from a later period.

Primary evidence

This may include:

- evidence written or produced at the time
- artefacts – e.g. goods or items such as pots, jewellery, armour, books, etc.
- archaeological evidence
- buildings
- drawings
- paintings
- photographs.

Secondary evidence

This may include:

- written evidence such as history text books
- artists' reconstructions.

The sources on these pages are examples of some of the different kinds of evidence that can help us to find out about life in Scotland in 1700.

Source A

Scotland had an estimated population of a little more than one million inhabitants. This was about one-fifth the population of England. Scotland was overwhelmingly a rural-based society. The produce of the land – skins, grain, wool and coal – was vital for trade and so the typical Scot was a country dweller. In 1700 only one person in twenty lived in towns with over 10,000 inhabitants.

From a modern history book published in 1999.

Source B

 The small town of Paisley in Renfrewshire, drawn around 1690. Paisley later became a cloth weaving centre (see page 35) and is now one of Scotland's larger towns.

Source C

The 'penny wedding'. Although this picture was painted towards the end of the eighteenth century, only the clothes would have been different in 1700. At a penny wedding, all the guests paid what they could towards the cost of their meal, and the bride and groom kept any money that was left over after the wedding had been paid for.

5

Source D

The council commands each family within the burgh to provide sufficient vessels in their houses for holding their excrements and water for at least 48 hours. The council also forbids anyone to throw any filth in chamber pots out of the windows at either the back or the front of the house.

From the records of Edinburgh burgh (town) council for 1701.

Source E

Playing at cards and dice in coffee houses, taverns and other public houses has been the occasion of horrid cursing, swearing, quarrelling, strife, drinking, loss of time, neglect of business and many other inconveniences, so playing at cards or dice is prohibited.

From the Edinburgh burgh records for 1704.

Source F

In the early eighteenth century there was scarcely any furniture in even the laird's house. The beds seem to have been the most important items, even in the best rooms, and they were generally box-beds, built like cupboards in the walls, where one or two guests could be shut away for the night if they stayed too long over their drink. A four-poster bed was still a novelty. It often occupied one of the downstairs rooms where a laird could receive his guests and show it off.

From a modern history of the Scottish people.

Source G

To cure childhood illness take a little black puppy, choke it, open it and take out the gall bladder, which hath not above three or four drops of pure choler; give it all to the child and you shall see him cured.

From a book of family medicine published in 1712.

Source H

▲ *Most Scots who lived in the country probably lived in cottages like these.*

Source I

The poorer people live in the most miserable huts I have ever seen. Men, women and children pig together in a poor mousehole of mud, heath and some such matter.

From the writings of Thomas Kirke, who visited Scotland in 1679.

6

Questions

1. Make a table to show the relevance of each of the sources of evidence. Identify each source; then give details as to whether it is primary or secondary evidence; and finally add what it tells us about Scottish life in 1700.

2. Using the evidence that you have collected, make a list of the conclusions you have reached about life in Scotland in 1700. You should have evidence for each of your conclusions.

3. What else would you need to know to understand Scottish life in 1700 more fully?

4. What other types of evidence might you use to find out what it was like to live in Scotland over 300 years ago?

2 The Jacobites and the Union

In 1714 Queen Anne died. Despite 17 pregnancies, none of her children lived for long and the British throne passed to a distant Protestant relative, George of Hanover, who was German. The Act of Union said that Scotland could not choose a different ruler from the person chosen by the British Parliament when Anne died. Moreover, the English Parliament insisted that the next ruler must be a member of the Church of England, as laid down in the English Act of Succession of 1701. In fact, Anne had a half-brother, James Francis Edward Stewart (see the royal family tree below), but he was not allowed to inherit the throne because he was a Catholic. As James claimed that he rightfully should be king, he was forced to live abroad – first in France and then later in Rome.

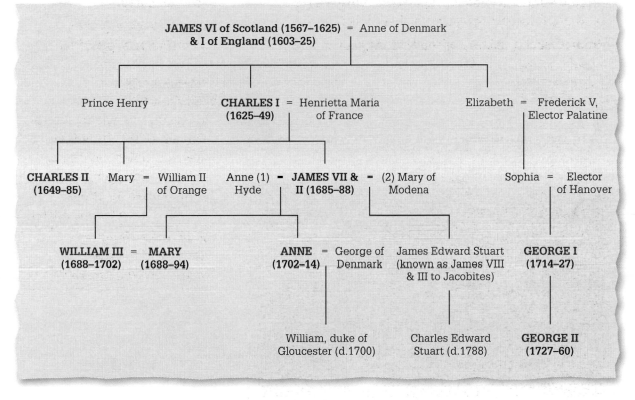

▲ *Kings and queens of Britain 1603–1760. Note that until 1707 the monarch was ruler of two separate kingdoms – Scotland and England.*

There were people in both Scotland and England who believed that James should be king. James's followers were known as Jacobites, named after *Jacobus*, the Latin name for James. They resented George I, whom they often referred to as 'the wee German lairdie'. Jacobites had already unsuccessfully attempted to win back the throne for the Stewarts in 1689 and 1708. Now, in 1715, they made a much more serious effort to restore James Stewart to the British throne.

—— Why did people support the Jacobites?

Many people in Scotland were unhappy about the Act of Union; supporting the Stewart claim to the throne was a way of showing how much they hated it. At the same time, the French, who were at war with Britain, realised that it might be to their advantage to provide some support for a Stewart attempt to regain the British throne. A Jacobite uprising would create problems for the British government and make it more difficult for them to fight in Europe.

Factfile – the 1715 uprising

- A leading Scot, the Earl of Mar, was refused a position in George I's government. He was furious and immediately became a Jacobite.

- In early August Mar left London and went north to start a Jacobite rebellion in Scotland. He hoped to gain support from the King of France.

- *6 September* Mar gathered an army of Jacobite supporters at Braemar. The king of France, Louis XIV, had died a few days earlier and the new French regent was not prepared to support the Jacobites.

- *14 September* Mar's Jacobite army of nearly 10,000 men took Perth.

- The Duke of Argyll led a government army towards Stirling, planning to stop Mar from reaching the Scottish Lowlands.

- Mar hesitated. A smaller Jacobite army crossed the Firth of Forth. This army joined up with English Jacobites and reached Preston, in the north of England, by November.

- English and Scottish Jacobites were unable to agree about where they should go next.

- *13 November* 6000 Jacobite soldiers under Mar's command fought 3000 of Argyll's men at Sheriffmuir. The battle was indecisive but Mar hesitated again and decided to retreat.

- On the same day, in the north of England, government troops forced the Jacobites at Preston to surrender.

- *22 December* James Stewart landed at Peterhead. His arrival had been delayed by bad weather.

- *February 1716* James Stewart and the Earl of Mar escaped by boat to France.

8

Source A

The Act of Union was not popular. The growing demand for money to pay for overseas wars resulted in tax increases or new taxes on necessities such as malt, salt and linen. The Jacobites could pose as the champions of Scottish nationalism and the defenders of Scottish liberty. 'No Union' became a common motto on Jacobite banners.

From a modern history book published in 1999.

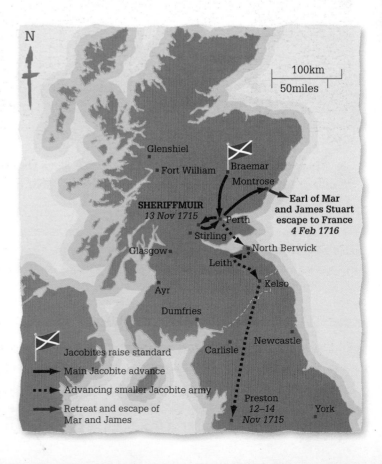

Map to show the movement of the armies during the 1715 uprising. ▶

Source B

Supporting the Jacobites was a way in which people could criticise the British government.

The view of a modern historian writing in 1980.

Source C

▲ *The execution of Lord Kenmure and Lord Derwentwater, two important English Jacobites. All but two of the prisoners taken after Preston were either pardoned or escaped from prison.*

Questions

1. Study the factfile carefully. Make a timeline to show the main events of the 1715 uprising.

2. Study the opinions of the two historians given in Sources A and B.
   How far do they agree about the reasons why many people supported the Jacobites?

3. Make a list of all the reasons you can find which help explain why the Jacobite uprising was unsuccessful.

4. Now write a paragraph explaining the failure of the 1715 uprising, beginning with the sentence, 'There are several reasons why the uprising of 1715 was unsuccessful'.

Scottish towns after the Union

The people who lived in Scottish towns were generally law-abiding. However, occasionally large crowds of people took to the streets to show their anger about something; in 1725 and 1736 there were riots over changes which were blamed on the Act of Union.

The malt tax riot in Glasgow, 1725

Large, angry crowds gathered to protest outside the house of the local MP, Daniel Campbell. Campbell supported a new government tax on malt, which meant the price of beer would increase. People in the crowd believed that the new tax had been introduced as a result of the Act of Union. Two companies of soldiers arrived to try to keep the peace and the crowds started to throw stones. Alarmed, the soldiers fired at the crowd, and continued to do so, even when they were ordered to retreat. At least nine people died in the confusion which followed. The London government believed that the town council had secretly encouraged the mob to riot and Glasgow was forced to pay large amounts of money as compensation for the damage done.

▲ *Artist's impression of the crowd rioting outside the Shawfields house of MP Daniel Campbell.*

Why did the people of Edinburgh riot in 1736?

The smuggler's hanging

Smuggling was common in the eighteenth century. It became more widespread in Scotland after the Act of Union, which brought an increase in the taxes on such goods as brandy and wine. Many people were able to obtain alcohol and other goods cheaply thanks to the activities of smugglers. Ports on the east coast of Scotland were famous for their smugglers, who avoided the unpopular customs officers and were admired by the local people.

In 1736 two well-known smugglers, George Robertson and Andrew Wilson, were imprisoned in the Edinburgh Tolbooth awaiting public execution. (The Tolbooth was a building which existed in most burghs for the collection of local taxes and was often used as a prison.) On the Sunday before they were to be hanged they were taken to church, so that all the townspeople could see them and be reminded of what happened to those who broke the law. As they sat in church, guarded by four soldiers, Robertson made a break for freedom; he jumped over the pews and escaped into the streets. None of the onlookers tried to stop him and he was never recaptured.

The following day Wilson, who had not escaped, was led to his execution in the Grassmarket, in front of a large crowd. As usual, the uniformed city guard were present. When the hanging took place people threw stones and there was some jeering, but there was no more violence than was usual. However, Captain Porteous, who was in charge of the city guard, ordered his men to fire. In the confusion which followed eight or nine people were killed and about 20 were wounded.

—— *The revenge of the crowd*

As a result, Captain Porteous was arrested, tried and sentenced to death. This verdict was popular in Edinburgh, where he was blamed for the shootings. Then came the news that

Porteous, who had been drinking, ordered his guard to fire. As their muskets were loaded with shot, the soldiers showed reluctance and I saw Porteous turn to them with a threatening gesture. They obeyed, and fired; but wishing to do as little harm as possible, many of them raised their muskets before they fired. Unfortunately, the effect of this was that some people were wounded in the windows which were crowded with onlookers and one unfortunate lad was killed.

An account written many years after the event by Alexander Carlyle, who witnessed the incident as a 14-year old.

Queen Caroline had ordered the execution to be postponed for six weeks. Porteous had friends in the right places! This was too much for the people of Edinburgh. They were angry about what they saw as interference from England and they resented the Act of Union, which they felt had made this kind of interference possible. On 7 September 1736 a large mob burned down the door of the Tolbooth where Porteous was held prisoner.

11

Source B

▲ *Edinburgh during the Porteous riots. This picture was painted in 1855, over 100 years after the riots.*

Although Porteous tried to escape up a chimney he became stuck and was dragged out to the Grassmarket where he was publicly hanged. The hanging had been carefully planned: the gates into the city were closed and there was complete silence so as not to alarm the military garrison in the castle. There was no other damage and the rioters even paid a guinea (£1.05) for the noose.

When the news of the execution of Captain Porteous reached London, there was fury about what had happened. All investigations into the affair were met with stony silence and the government fined the city of Edinburgh £2000.

Questions

1. In your own words, describe what happened in Edinburgh in 1736.

2. Copy the headings below and use them to record your findings. The first entry has been done for you. Then draw lines to join up all the similarities between the two riots.

Glasgow 1725	Edinburgh 1736
People were angry about taxes.	Smugglers were popular because they helped people avoid taxes.

3. Source A is from an eye witness account of the Porteous riots. Source B was painted more than 100 years later. The artist, who lived in Edinburgh, was very interested in history.

   How useful are Sources A and B as evidence of what happened during the Porteous riots? For each source, you should think about:

   a. Who produced it?

   b. When and why was it produced?

   c. What does it tell us?

   d. Is it likely to be accurate?

4. What do the riots in Glasgow and Edinburgh reveal about attitudes towards the Union in the first half of the eighteenth century?

4 The Jacobite challenge in 1745

Although the 1715 uprising failed, there were still people who hoped that a Stewart would once again sit on the British throne. In the meantime, James VIII of Scotland and III of England – as he was known to his supporters – lived in Rome, surrounded by his Jacobite court. To his opponents he was known as The Pretender, meaning claimant to the throne. In 1720 James' wife gave birth to a son, Charles Edward (see the royal family tree on page 7). Living in the Mutti Palace in Rome, and surrounded by Jacobite supporters, the young prince never questioned the Stewart claim to the British throne. In his eyes, it was just a matter of time before he would lead an uprising and declare his father King of Great Britain.

Source A

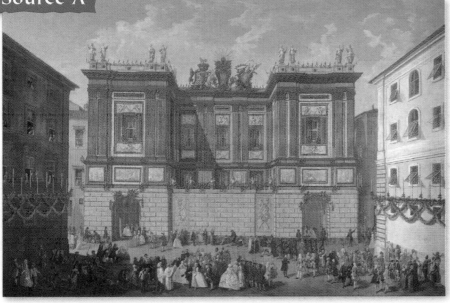

◀ *James Stewart and his court at the Mutti Palace in Rome.*

How strong was Jacobite support in Scotland?

Visitors to the Stewart court in Rome encouraged the prince to believe that there were plenty of Jacobite supporters in England and Scotland. But Britain had changed considerably by the time that Charles Edward was old enough to think realistically of organising a Jacobite uprising.

By 1740 the British government seemed to have more control over Jacobite areas in the Highlands of Scotland than they had had in 1715. General Wade had overseen the building of new roads and bridges throughout the Highlands. This meant that troops were moved around the country more easily when the need arose. New forts were built at Fort Augustus and Bernera while existing garrisons at Fort William and Ruthven were strengthened, so there were plenty of government soldiers stationed in Scotland to deal with emergencies.

Many people in the Lowlands were beginning to enjoy the advantages of freer trade with England (see page 4). As a result, opposition to the Act of Union and to the British government was no longer seen as a reason for supporting the Stewarts.

In England, although there remained some people who disliked the Hanoverians, few were prepared to take part in an uprising against the monarchy. Only in some of the Highland clans and among Catholics and Episcopalians – who did not agree with the Church of Scotland – was there still much support for the Pretender.

From 1738 onwards, however, Britain was at war with its European neighbours. This had two important consequences for the Jacobites. Firstly, the government removed many soldiers from the Scottish forts and sent them to fight abroad. Secondly, and more importantly, since Britain and France were at war, it seemed likely that the French government would support a Jacobite invasion of Britain. Causing trouble for the British at home would distract them from the fighting in Europe.

Source B

By the 1740s Jacobitism was unpopular throughout most of the Lowlands. Glasgow and the towns in the west of Scotland were resolutely opposed to it. Church of Scotland clergymen played up fears that the return of the Stewarts would mean a return to Catholicism in Scotland.

From a modern history book published in 1999.

The Prince has come home!

In 1744 Prince Charles Edward Stewart travelled from Rome to Paris. The French king had decided to provide 10,000 troops to support a Jacobite invasion of Britain. As the older son of James VIII, Prince Charles would lead the invading forces and claim the British throne for his father. Unfortunately for the Jacobites, severe gales made it impossible for the French troops to cross the English Channel and the invasion plans were eventually called off.

Frustrated by what had happened, Prince Charles decided to go ahead without the French. He hoped that once he landed in Britain the French would provide the support that he needed. His supporters in Scotland warned him that he could not succeed without French weapons, money and troops but he ignored their warnings. In July 1745 Charles Edward Stewart and seven companions landed in the Outer Hebrides.

Support gathers for the Prince

At first even those Highland chiefs who were Jacobites were reluctant to support the Prince. Some, however, promised their support, most notably Cameron of Lochiel and Macdonald of Clanranald. This was important because it was the clan chief who called on the men of the clan to fight. On 18 August Prince Charles landed on the Scottish mainland at Glenfinnan (see map on page 16) and raised the Jacobite standard, or flag, as a sign that the rebellion had begun. By the end of the day, he had been joined by about 1200 clansmen.

Because Britain was fighting a war in Europe, there were few government soldiers to defend Scotland against the Jacobites. When it was clear that there was a real threat of another Jacobite uprising, General Sir John Cope was ordered to gather together government troops and destroy the rebel army. Cope knew that his troops were not experienced and that if they fought the rebels in the Highlands the Jacobites would have an advantage, since the clansmen were more skilled at fighting in hilly country. He decided to avoid a battle and marched his army, first to Inverness and then to Aberdeen. This left the way open for Prince Charles's army to head for Stirling and the Lowlands.

Edinburgh falls to Prince Charles

On 16 September 1745 the Jacobites were just outside Edinburgh. The government troops who had been left to guard the city fled in disorder when the Jacobite army fired a few shots. Prince Charles demanded that the city should surrender and, by nightfall, the Jacobites had taken Edinburgh without a single casualty. The following day Prince Charles Edward Stewart rode in triumph through the city and took up residence in Holyrood Palace, proclaiming his father, James, to be king.

The population of a great city, who cheer at anything that brings them together, cheered; and a number of ladies in the windows strained their voices shouting and waved white handkerchiefs in honour of the day. Few gentlemen were to be seen on the streets or in the windows.

An eyewitness description of the scenes in Edinburgh when James VIII was proclaimed king.

The Battle of Prestonpans

For the government, worse news was to come. On 21 September Jacobite soldiers managed to make a surprise attack on Cope's army, which had been transported by sea from Aberdeen to the Firth of Forth. Having made their way at night across a boggy marsh outside Prestonpans, the Highlanders took Cope's men by surprise. The Highlanders's wild attack with broadswords and scythes fastened to poles terrrified Cope's inexperienced men and the government army was defeated in less than 15 minutes. Rebel casualties were few, but they killed about 300 of Cope's soldiers and took about 1500 prisoners.

Source D

▲ *After the Battle of Prestonpans General Cope and the remnants of his army fled south. Cope, on the right horse, is shown reaching Berwick with the news of his defeat. The figure standing at the town gate is clearly not amused that the general has fled to safety ahead of his troops, and comments that this is the first time that he has heard of a general bringing the news of his own defeat.*

The Jacobites were victorious, but Prince Charles said 'he was far from rejoicing at the death of any of his father's subjects'. Even anti-Jacobites admitted that the injured and prisoners were treated with great compassion by Prince Charles.

15

—— *Indecision and delay*

Prince Charles spent another six weeks in Edinburgh. The size of the Jacobite army increased as more Highlanders and a few Lowlanders arrived. But the new supporters were fewer than expected and the Jacobites were short of money so burghs throughout Scotland were forced to pay taxes. Most important of all, the delay meant that the British government had time to recall troops from Europe so that they could be used in the fight against the Jacobites.

The Jacobites were divided about what to do next. Prince Charles wanted to invade England, believing that once his army crossed the border, English Jacobites would join them. The Highland chiefs, however, doubted the strength of English support and thought that their forces were too small to fight government troops. Eventually the Prince's council voted in favour of invasion with a majority of one vote, and on 1 November 1745 the Jacobite army left Edinburgh and headed south.

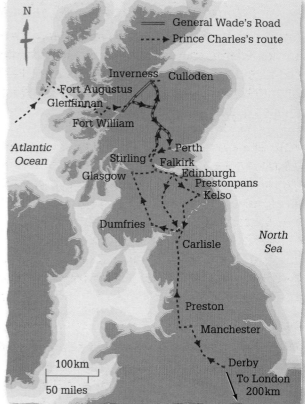

The movement of the ▲
Jacobite armies 1745–6.

┌ Questions ──────

1. What can we learn from Source A on page 13 about the Stewart court in exile?

2. Why had Scottish support for the Jacobites declined since 1715?

3. 'By 1745, there was little chance that a Jacobite uprising would be successful.'

   a. What evidence can you find which supports this view?

   b. What evidence can you find which does not support this view? Write your answers under two appropriate headings.

4. Explain why the Jacobites were successful between August and November 1745 although they did not have a large army. In your answer you should consider:

   a. the Jacobites's advantages

   b. the weaknesses of the government forces.

5. Do you think that the author of Source C on page 15 supported the Jacobites? Read the source carefully and refer to what the author said in your answer.

6. Look at Source D on page 15. What did the cartoonist who drew this picture want people to think about General Cope?

Why were the Jacobites defeated at Culloden?

When the Jacobite army invaded England, many of the 5000 Highlanders who marched south believed that they would be joined by English supporters of the Stewarts. They also believed that, within a few weeks, Prince Charles's father, James, would be proclaimed king in London, as had already happened in Edinburgh (see page 15).

'The Jacobites are coming!'

At first the Jacobites made good progress. Carlisle surrendered to them on 15 November 1745 and a fortnight later the Jacobites reached Manchester. Avoiding government troops, the Jacobite army reached Derby on 4 December. London was only 204 km (126 miles) away. No Scottish army had advanced so far into England and there was panic in the capital. On hearing the rumours that 'ferocious and barbarian' Highlanders were about to reach London, shops closed and people rushed to the banks to try to withdraw their savings. There were large numbers of government troops to defend the city but many were untrained and people feared that they would be no match for the Highlanders's terrifying battle tactics.

However, the Jacobite army was not as strong as many in England feared. Only a few hundred English Jacobites had joined them – not the thousands that Prince Charles had hoped for. Also, there was still no sign of French support, although the Prince remained convinced that French troops would arrive once the Jacobite army reached London. Meanwhile General Wade and the Duke of Cumberland marched to the defence of London with two more government armies. It seemed that the Jacobites would be heavily outnumbered.

Retreat

In Derby the Jacobite leaders held a meeting with the Prince. Lord George Murray, who commanded the Jacobite army, insisted that they should retreat. Prince Charles was astounded but he could not persuade Murray to change his mind. And so, in the depths of winter, the poorly-equipped Highland army started to return to Scotland.

By 20 December the Jacobites were back in Scotland, but by the time that they reached Glasgow nearly a third of the original army had deserted. In January 1746 they were joined by more Jacobite supporters in Scotland and succeeded in defeating poorly-led government troops at the battle of Falkirk.

Source E

As soon as the Highlanders found that we were retracing our steps, nothing was to be heard throughout the whole Jacobite army but expressions of rage and lamentation.

From the memoirs of a Jacobite officer, writing about the retreat from Derby in December 1745.

Source F

The junior officers of the prince's army were much surprised when they found the army moving back but when they were told everything they blamed their superiors much for carrying them so far, and approved much of going back to Scotland.

From the memoirs of Lord Elcho, one of the leaders of the Jacobite army returning to Scotland from Derby.

17

The British government now sent the Duke of Cumberland, the 24-year-old son of King George II, to take charge of the government forces. Again the Jacobite leaders thought it best to retreat, believing that their best chance of victory was in the Highlands. By the time they reached Inverness, most of the Jacobites were dispirited, hungry and exhausted.

The Battle of Culloden, April 1746

By this time, the Duke of Cumberland was in Aberdeen with about 9000 troops, including many Scots. In April he moved his army towards Inverness. The Jacobites, now down to about 5000 men, expected an immediate attack and gathered on Drumossie Moor, Culloden, on 15 April 1746. Lord George Murray saw that the flat, open moorland would make it easier for the government troops to win, and suggested a surprise night attack on Cumberland's army, which was by then 19km (12 miles) away at Nairn. This plan did not work out, however, and the Highlanders returned to Culloden early the following morning, exhausted by a long night march which had achieved nothing.

Source G

▲ *The fighting at Culloden, painted in 1746. Jacobite prisoners were used to pose for the artist.*

18

At around midday on 16 April Cumberland's redcoats opened fire on the Jacobites, who were about 300 metres away. The Highlanders were mown down by cannon shot. Eventually, in desperation, they decided to charge at the government troops. This time the Highland charge across the flat moor proved ineffective. The government troops now knew how to contain the Jacobite charge and the Highlanders were cut down by rounds of musket shot as they advanced. When the Highlanders were close enough to raise their traditional Highland broadswords, the government redcoats used the bayonets fixed to their muskets to stab their opponents to death. The battle was over in less than half an hour.

Questions

1. Make a timeline to show the main events of the Jacobite uprising of 1745–6.

2. Sources E and F were both written after 1745 by men who held important positions in the Jacobite army.

   a. Why do you think that the two men differ so much in their reactions to the decision to retreat from Derby?

   b. What does this suggest about the way in which historians should use primary source evidence?

3. Source G was painted in 1746 but the artist was not present at the battle.

   a. What do you notice about how the artist has painted the soldiers on the two different sides?

   b. How useful is the painting as evidence of what happened at Culloden?

Extended writing

1. Explain why the Jacobite uprising of 1745–6 resulted in the defeat at Culloden.

   To answer this question fully:

   a. consider what had happened before the battle

   b. consider what happened on the battlefield itself.

   You could present your answer as a newspaper front-page story covering the battle.

   Visit the school library to find out more about what happened during the battle.

5 The results of the Jacobite uprising

Prince Charles's army may have been defeated at Culloden in less than half an hour, but the results of the Jacobite defeat were long-lasting and changed the Highlands forever. The battle itself, and what happened in the following months, left a legacy of hatred and suspicion that would remain for many years.

—— Cumberland terrorises the Highlands

At the end of the Battle of Culloden, government soldiers ruthlessly murdered most of the wounded Highlanders and many more Highlanders were killed as they tried to flee the battlefield. Innocent local people were also killed as Cumberland's troops pursued the Highlanders towards Inverness. From the Duke of Cumberland's point of view, the Highlanders were traitors who had supported a rebellion against the king, and as traitors they deserved to be treated with brutality.

Source A

Drive away the cattle, burn the ploughs and destroy what you can belonging to all such as are, or have been in the rebellion, and burn the houses of the chiefs.

Government orders given after the Battle of Culloden.

Encouraged by Cumberland, government troops (including those Scots who had fought in the government army) destroyed Highlanders's homes and burned their crops. Cattle were stolen and families which were suspected of supporting the Jacobites were forced to leave their land. Without food or shelter, many children and old people died. In the three months after the battle, many Highlanders were murdered and over 3000 prisoners were taken.

Meanwhile Prince Charles was on the run and in hiding. In September 1746 he finally escaped to France and never returned to Britain. He died in Rome over 40 years later, a bitter and disappointed man.

Case Study – What did the government do to prevent another Jacobite rebellion?

- Fort George was built near Inverness to strengthen government defences. At the time it was one of the most formidable fortresses in all of Europe.

- The Jacobite leaders were executed for treason and nearly 1000 men were transported overseas.

- The powers of the Highland chiefs were greatly reduced to destroy clan loyalties, particularly the tradition that clansmen were obliged to follow their clan chief into battle.

- Those chiefs who had played an important part in the uprising had their land taken away and commissioners were appointed to run their estates. These commissioners believed that it was their duty to modernise the Highlands by destroying the old Highland way of life. The commissioners improved agriculture and communications, and tried to bring greater employment to the area.

- For nearly 40 years it was forbidden to wear tartan or to play the bagpipes.

20

'Bonnie Prince Charlie' – the legend

After 1745 Highlanders were treated with great suspicion. They were regarded as backward and uncivilised people who behaved like savages (see Source B). Jacobites were thought to be dangerous enemies who posed a real threat to security. But as time passed it became clear that there was no threat of another uprising, so people forgot these feelings. By the beginning of the nineteenth century, the uprising of 1745 started to fascinate authors like Sir Walter Scott. Charles Edward Stewart and the Jacobites were shown as romantic figures, and tartan and bagpipes came to be regarded not just as symbols of the Highlands but as harmless symbols of Scottish identity. The actual events of 1745–6 were forgotten and the myth of 'Bonnie Prince Charlie' was born. The Jacobites were no longer seen as a dangerous threat to the government but as tragic, brave men who were fighting for a hopeless cause. Stories about Prince Charles' adventures after Culloden became popular and artists portrayed both the Prince and his supporters in a way that was intended to make people think favourably of the Jacobites (see Source C on page 22).

Source B

◄ *A cartoon published in 1745. The Highlander is shown as so ignorant that he does not know how to use the standard boghouse, or toilet. Two-seater toilets were clearly common then!*

Source C

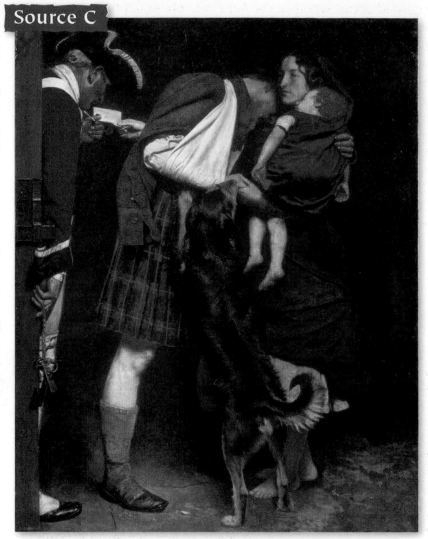

◀ *A romanticised nineteenth-century painting showing a Jacobite soldier reunited with his family. This picture is typical of the way in which Victorian artists portrayed Jacobite supporters.*

Questions

1. Describe what happened after the Battle of Culloden.

2. 'A deliberate attempt to destroy the Highland way of life.'

   a. What evidence can you find to support this view of the changes in the Highlands after 1746?

   b. Can you suggest any other reasons why life in the Highlands changed in the second half of the eighteenth century?

3. Study Sources B and C.

   a. What did the artist who drew Source B want people to think?

   b. What was the point of view of the artist who painted Source C?

   c. Why do you think that attitudes towards the Jacobites had changed so much by the nineteenth century?

6 The Union: fifty years on

In 1707 Scots had been bitterly divided about whether the Act of Union would benefit Scotland. Some of those who opposed the Union supported the Jacobites in 1715 and 1745. Others joined in with the rioting in Glasgow in 1725 and in Edinburgh in 1736. Gradually, however, opposition to the Act of Union grew less. Was this because the Act of Union had made Scotland a more prosperous country?

Better farming

The Act of Union allowed Scots to sell their produce in England. New opportunities were created for landowners, who found that there was a growing demand for Scottish cattle and grain south of the border. Many of the wealthiest Scottish landowners now spent part of the year in London, where life was much more expensive than in Scotland, so they looked for new ways to make money. Some landowners raised their tenants's rents, and some even evicted tenants in order to create larger farms which could produce more cattle, oats and barley for the English market. Others realised that they could increase their income if they farmed the land more efficiently and started to look for ways of improving farming methods. Over time, these new ways of farming were copied widely and more food was produced in Scotland.

Linen and tobacco markets boom

Some industries were at first badly affected by the Union. Producers of Scottish linen and woollen cloth were hit hard by competition with England, as were those involved in brewing and papermaking. By the 1740s, however, the linen trade had recovered. Incentives were introduced to encourage producers to export more linen and as a result there were huge increases in the amount of Scottish linen sold to England and to the British colonies in North America and the Caribbean.

Scottish merchants who took advantage of the right to trade with Britain's colonies across the Atlantic gained the most. Before the Act of Union, Scots had not been allowed to trade with England's colonies. Now Scottish merchants benefited from trans-Atlantic trade. In particular, Glasgow merchants developed a flourishing trade in North American tobacco. Historians now believe that the early Scottish tobacco traders were particularly successful because they were expert 'smugglers'! Merchants made deals with customs officials so that only some of the tobacco they imported into Scotland was taxed. This meant that they were able to undercut the price of tobacco imported by English merchants.

23

Source A

The Union opened the door to the Scots in our American colonies and the Glasgow merchants took up the opportunity. I am assured that they send nearly fifty ships every year to Virginia and other English colonies in America.

Daniel Defoe, an Englishman, writing in 1726 after a visit to Glasgow.

Source B

Even the toughest frontiers of the empire attracted men of first-rate ability from Scotland because they were usually poorer than their English counter-parts with fewer prospects of success in Britain.

A modern historian writing in 1992.

The Union: fifty years on

The pull of new foreign markets

The Union also meant that Scottish merchants and skilled tradesmen emigrated. Some went to North America or to the West Indies, hoping to make sufficient money to buy a few slaves and set up a business out there. Many others went to India, hoping to make a fortune working for the East India Company. Some of these men returned home at the end of their careers abroad, bringing back with them a sizeable fortune to invest in farming, or in building roads to open up new areas within Scotland. Others were less successful; some died overseas of disease or in poverty.

Glasgow and the tobacco lords

Anyone visiting Glasgow around 1760 and going to the Trongate (one of the main streets and a prominent feature of the city centre) at midday, would almost certainly have come across several of the 'tobacco lords' – the leading Glasgow merchants – discussing the affairs of the day. These wealthy men had made their money by importing tobacco from North America.

Glasgow's share of the trade in tobacco grew rapidly after the Union with England. By 1770 almost half of all the tobacco imported from America into Britain went through Glasgow. Much of it was re-exported to France. The distance between Glasgow and Virginia – where most of the tobacco was grown – was slightly shorter than the distance between the main English ports and North America. The Glasgow merchants used this to their advantage and, by 1760, the wealthiest 'tobacco lords' owned their own ships and were investing in the most up-to-date technology to speed up the trans-Atlantic journey as much as possible.

The tobacco lords

Dressed in scarlet cloaks and satin suits, wearing powdered wigs and three-cornered hats, and carrying gold-topped canes, the 'lords' met daily at the Trongate. Their servants followed them, smartly dressed in breeches, with brass buttons on their coats and gold bands on their hats.

These merchants could afford to sell tobacco more cheaply than English merchants. This was because they had established an efficient 'store' system in America. Factors (agents) working in Virginia set up stores in the tobacco-producing colonies. Tobacco growers could obtain supplies of the goods that they needed from these stores. As they were often short of cash, the agent let them have the goods on credit, on the understanding that they would sell him their next tobacco crop. The planters liked the 'store system' because they often received a better price for their tobacco if they obtained their supplies from the factor's store.

As far as the factors were concerned, the system enabled them to purchase large supplies of tobacco so that when ships arrived from Glasgow they could be loaded up as fast as possible for the return voyage. The 'store system' meant that the tobacco lords' ships made several trans-Atlantic voyages each year. Using the same ship for several voyages each year kept transport costs down and the tobacco could be sold at a lower price.

What did the tobacco lords do with the money they made?

- Some merchants built themselves fine town houses near the centre of Glasgow.

- Others purchased large estates outside the city because the possession of land demonstrated the owner's important position in society, and also brought an income from lettings to tenant farmers.

- Some tobacco lords were interested in introducing new, more profitable farming methods.

- Others invested in mining to extract the coal which lay beneath their land.

- In 1752 tobacco lords set up Glasgow's first banks. The bank notes which these early banks issued helped to increase trade, and the money deposited in these banks was often used to help finance new industries.

- Several tobacco lords invested in the Monklands Canal which was later used to transport coal from Lanarkshire to Glasgow.

- Many tobacco merchants set up businesses to manufacture goods which were sold in their 'stores' in Virginia and elsewhere in the colonies. They produced rope and sailcloth, leather and textiles, and set up printing presses, glassworks and iron works. One tobacco merchant invested in no less than 17 different small businesses!

Source C

25

▲ *A tobacco lord smoking a pipe and enjoying the luxurious life provided by the profits he has made from tobacco. Notice that slaves were used to grow American tobacco.*

Tobacco imports into Glasgow before and after the American Declaration of Independence (1776)	
Year	amount of tobacco imported (in millions of lbs)
1715	2.5
1728	7.25
1771	47.25
1777	0.3

Source D

When a merchant has been successful, he purchases a piece of land, builds an elegant villa and improves his property at the dearest rates.

The Old Statistical Account. *This important document was published in the 1790s. A Scottish landowner, Sir John Sinclair, wrote to every church minister in Scotland and asked for information about their local areas. Almost all of the ministers replied and the* Old Statistical Account *is based on the information that they provided.*

Questions

1. Identify two groups of Scots who benefited from the Union. Explain why each of these groups prospered after 1707.

2. In your own words, explain why the tobacco lords were important in eighteenth-century Glasgow.

3. Study the table of tobacco imports into Glasgow.

   a. Draw a bar graph to illustrate the tobacco trade between 1715 and 1777.

   b. Try to find out why imports fell in 1777.

Extended writing

1. 'The Act of Union only benefited those who had money. Poorer people did not benefit at all.'
   How far do you agree with this statement?
   You should provide a balanced answer to this question:

   a. Start your answer: 'Many of the richer people in Scotland benefited from the Union…'
      Then you should mention several different groups of wealthy people and explain why, and in what ways, they benefited.

   b. Start your second paragraph: 'Poorer people did not benefit so much…' and give some examples. However, you should also consider whether there was more food to eat and more jobs available.

   c. Having considered both sides of the argument, write a balanced conclusion to the answer.

2. Imagine that you are a wealthy tobacco lord who has just had a very successful year. Write a letter to a fellow merchant explaining what you intend to do with the profits you have made. You may want to consider several options before reaching a conclusion.

26

> *On stair wi' tub or pat[1] in hand*
>
> *The barefoot housemaids looe[2] to stand*
>
> *That antrin fock[3] may ken how snell[4]*
>
> *Auld Reekie wil at morning smell:*
>
> *Then with an inundation big as*
>
> *The burn that 'neath the Nor Loch Brig is,*
>
> *They kindly shower Edina's roses[5]*
>
> *To quicken and regale our noses.*

[1] pot [2] love [3] passers by [4] pungent, strong smelling
[5] household slops thrown out on to the street

Robert Fergusson, the Edinburgh poet who wrote this poem (published in 1773), was describing a well-known aspect of life in eighteenth-century Edinburgh. After ten o'clock at night people were allowed to throw their household waste out into the streets. As there were no flush toilets, the contents of the 'close stool', which was kept in the house during the day, were thrown out with the rest of the household waste. The cry of 'gardy-loo' (from the French, *Prenez-garde à l'eau*, meaning 'Beware of the water!') was not always a sufficient warning; for some passers-by the reply 'Haud yer hand' may have come too late as they hurried home through unlit streets!

Robert Fergusson knew all about what he called 'Edina's roses', as he was born in 1750 in a close just off the High Street. The city in which he grew up had changed little since the Middle Ages. There were just two main streets which were connected by narrow 'wynds', or lanes. The old city walls stood to the east, south and west, while the stagnant and polluted Nor' Loch marked the northern boundary. The only way to house the city's rapidly increasing population was to build upwards and some of the 'lands', or tenements, were 14 storeys high.

By 1750 it was clear that something had to be done to improve the city. The draining of the Nor' Loch began in 1759 and then, in 1766, the Lord Provost organised a competition to find the best plan to develop the uninhabited area to the north of the city.

Source A

Excrement lies in heaps in the streets. In the morning the scent was so offensive that we were forced to hold our noses and take care where we trod for fear of disobliging our shoes.

A visitor to Edinburgh in 1705.

Source B

We supped in a tavern and were very merry till the clock struck ten, when everybody is at liberty to throw their filth out of the window. The people in the tavern began to light pieces of paper and throw them upon the table to smoke the room and, as I thought, to mix one bad smell with another. When I was in bed I was forced to hide my head between the sheets for the smell of the filth came pouring into the room to such a degree, I was almost poisoned with the stench.

A visitor to Edinburgh commenting in 1754.

James Craig was the eventual winner, with a plan for a 'New Town' in complete contrast to the 'Old Town'. The streets would be broad and straight and the houses would provide suitable spacious accommodation for the wealthy middle classes of Edinburgh. By 1820 Edinburgh's New Town was growing fast. As it was mainly built during the reign of King George III, it is often referred to as the 'Georgian' New Town.

Source C

The dining room in a New Town house. The houses in the New Town had spacious rooms which were used for entertaining. ▶

28

— What was Edinburgh's 'Golden Age'?

Towards the end of the eighteenth century, it was not just the appearance of the city that changed. The years between 1760 and 1790 are often called Edinburgh's 'Golden Age'. Around 1700, visitors had considered Scotland to be a very poor and rather backward country. Sixty years later Scots were admired throughout Europe for their achievements in science, engineering, education, economics, philosophy, art and architecture. Edinburgh University was famed for the brilliance of its professors. Lawyers and doctors, writers and scientists, met together in clubs and societies to discuss new ideas. Many of them were also innovators and put their new ideas into practice.

Whatever their interests, these men shared certain common beliefs. They rejected ideas which were based on superstition, or which were accepted simply because people had believed them in the past. They thought that people could use their intelligence and reason to change the world and their lives for the better.

Source D

After 1750 Scotland was a more secure place in which to live. The Union with England was taken for granted and the Highlands were under firm government control. Rebellions were a thing of the past and men could turn all their energy into peaceful channels such as scientific and artistic developments. Recent improvements in farming meant that Scots now had enough food to eat. Housing was also getting better. Intolerance and religious quarrels were on the decline. People felt freer to put forward new ideas and to defend them in books and lectures.

From a modern history book published in 1985.

How do historians explain the 'Golden Age'?

Historians do not always agree about why the 'Golden Age' occurred. Some historians believe that life was more peaceful and settled after the Union and so there was more time for scientific and other intellectual pastimes. Other historians, however, think that the origins of the new ideas are to be found in Scottish society long before the Union with England took place.

Source E

The roots of 'the Golden Age' lay deep in the seventeenth century. New ideas had been gathering momentum in the universities since at least the 1670s and there had been considerable advances in the study of mathematics, law and some of the sciences from that time onwards. Despite appearances, continuity was more important than change.

From a modern history book published in 1992.

Source F

Here I stand at what is called the cross of Edinburgh (in the heart of the Old Town) and can, in a few minutes, take fifty men of genius and learning by the hand.

A visitor to Edinburgh commenting in about 1760.

Case study – Edinburgh's Clubs

Clubs were popular meeting places in Edinburgh during the 'Golden Age'. Their names suggest that these clubs were not always very serious. There was the Pious Club, whose members met to eat pies, and the Dirty Club, whose members were not allowed to wear clean clothes. At the Boar Club members were referred to as boars and the room where they met was called the sty. Talking was known as grunting! Another famous club was called the Poker Club because the members wanted to 'stir up' discussion about controversial topics. These clubs often met in taverns and much hard drinking took place.

Source G

This contemporary drawing suggests that Edinburgh clubs were not always very serious meeting places! ▶

Did women play any part in this 'Golden Age'?

In 1750 only about 25 per cent of Scottish women could write their own name. Middle and upper class girls were reasonably educated, however, although they did not study the same subjects as their brothers. We know that some of these women did follow the new ideas. At one series of public lectures women made up half of the audience, and women played a part in the renewed interest in art, music and singing. But for the most part even these educated women played a relatively small role in Edinburgh's 'Golden Age'.

Questions

1. At first people were reluctant to move into the New Town. Write four sentences explaining the benefits of the New Town to persuade wealthy people to live there. You should mention:

   a. the disadvantages of the Old Town

   b. the advantages of the New Town.

2. Explain what is meant by Edinburgh's 'Golden Age'.

3. Read the views of the two historians given in Sources D and E.

   a. What is the main point made in Source D?

   b. What is the main point made in Source E?

   c. Write a few sentences explaining how the views of the two historians differ.

4. Why are these people famous?

David Hume	Robert Adam
Adam Smith	James Hutton
Henry Raeburn	Robert Burns
Joseph Black	

   Prepare a short report on one of these famous Scotsmen associated with the 'Golden Age'.

   You will need to:

   - identify possible sources of information: for example, you could use a CD-Rom or the Internet, or you could look in the school or History department library

   - collect information from a range of primary and secondary sources (look back to page 4)

   - make a list of your findings and a plan of how best to present them

   - reach a conclusion about why the work of your famous Scotsman is still remembered today.

The Industrial Revolution

In the mid-eighteenth century, despite the growth of Edinburgh and Glasgow, most Scots lived and worked in the countryside. Yet just over 100 years later, more people lived in towns than in the countryside. Scotland, like England and Wales, had become an urban society. This gradual movement of thousands of people from the countryside to the towns had a huge effect on people's lives: on health, on housing, on family life and on leisure. Many of these changes brought great benefits to the Scottish people in the long run, but they also led to serious problems and suffering.

The term 'Industrial Revolution' is used to describe the period from about 1760 to 1830. A revolution is a period of great change. Most historians agree that the changes which took place in Scotland's industries at this time were revolutionary because they led to so many other changes in people's lives. Although most of Scotland's industries changed dramatically during the Industrial Revolution, it was the textile industry that changed first.

The Industrial Revolution 1 – what happened to spinning?

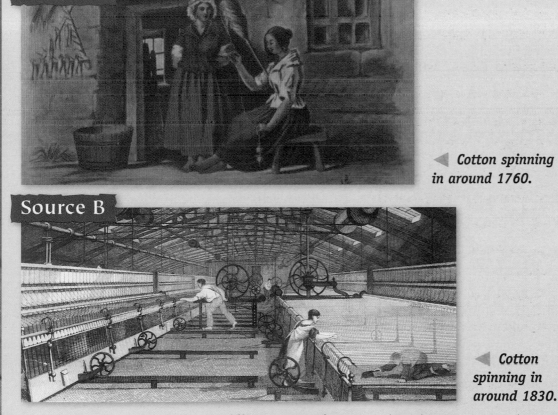

Case study – cotton spinning

Source A

◀ *Cotton spinning in around 1760.*

Source B

◀ *Cotton spinning in around 1830.*

Sources A and B illustrate two very different ways of spinning thread, or yarn. In each case, the spun yarn was woven into cloth, and possibly dyed or printed. In 1760 Scotland already produced significant amounts of wool and linen cloth, and all of the yarn used to produce this cloth was spun at home in conditions similar to those shown in Source A. Source B shows how yarn was spun by about 1830. By this time Scotland was producing large quantities of cotton cloth as well as wool and linen.

Questions

1. Read the case study on page 31. Now copy the headings and questions below and fill in your answers.

	Source A	Source B
How is yarn being produced?		
Where was the yarn being produced?		
What other differences can you see?		

2. Using the information from your table, write a paragraph about the changes that took place in textile production during the Industrial Revolution.

Cotton arrives from America – the growth of the mills

The invention of new spinning machines meant that yarn could be spun more quickly and more cheaply. At the same time, Glasgow's merchants started to import raw cotton from America and cotton cloth soon proved to be cheaper and easier to manufacture than either wool or linen. Spinning mills, powered by water, were built near fast-flowing rivers so that the weight of the water was used to drive the mill wheels.

The very first cotton spinning mill opened in 1778; within 20 years there were 95 cotton mills in Scotland, mainly in the west. After 1800 mill owners started to introduce steam power to drive the spinning machines. This meant that mills no longer had to be built near rivers but could be built in towns, where workers lived close to their work.

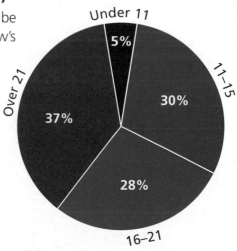

The age of mill workers taken from a survey made in 1834 ▲

Source C

When I went to a spinning mill I was about seven years old. I had to get out of bed every morning at five o'clock, begin work at half-past five, stop at nine for breakfast, begin again at half-past nine, work until two, which was the dinner hour. I started again at half-past two, and continued until half-past seven at night. The clocks in the factory were often put forward in the morning and back at night. Though all the workers knew this happened, they were afraid to say anything about it.

John Myles, a Dundee mill worker who wrote in 1850 about life as a factory boy.

Source D

I had one young girl under my charge at Dundee who could not see very well. Towards the evening she was sleepy and her thumb came into contact with the machinery. I was about three or four metres away from her when I heard the snap, and by the time that I came up, her thumb was away from her hand, and so she held out her hand to me with the thumb missing.

From John Myles' book about factory life published in 1850.

Questions

1. 'Very young children often went to work in the mills.'

   How far does the evidence in the pie chart agree with this statement?

2. Make a list of the evidence in Sources C and D which suggests that working conditions in mills were often harsh.

3. What reason do you think the mill owners would have given for the long hours that people had to work in their mills?

Why were the mills at New Lanark so famous?

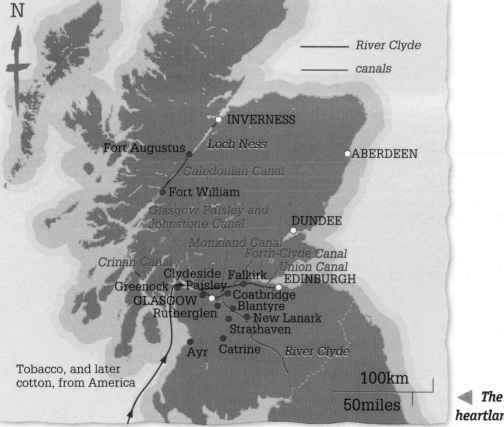

The new industrial heartland of Scotland.

In 1783 two men made a survey of the River Clyde near Lanark. One of them, David Dale, was a Glasgow businessman who already owned mills at Catrine in Ayrshire and at Blantyre in Lanarkshire. His English companion, Richard Arkwright, had invented the first water-powered spinning machine. They had come to see if the River Clyde near Lanark would be a suitable site for a spinning mill.

Within a year Dale and Arkwright had bought land beside the river and were building the largest cotton-spinning mill in Britain. The partnership did not last, however, and New Lanark belonged to David Dale when it opened in 1786. By 1793 there were over 1200 employees working there, many of them children.

Many of the children who worked at New Lanark were orphans from Edinburgh or Glasgow. With no family to look after them, the local parish had to find a way of providing for them. This was expensive, so the orphans were found work as young as possible. When they came to New Lanark it was agreed that they would not receive wages, but that David Dale would provide them with food, clothing and a basic education in return for their labour. This was a fairly common arrangement and few people thought that it was wrong to employ children in this way. In fact, David Dale was praised for the way in which he treated his child workers because conditions at New Lanark were better than in most other mills.

Young workers at New Lanark in 1793	
Age	Number of workers
6	5
7	33
8	71
9	95
10–11	over 200

Conditions in David Dale's mill

In 1796 David Dale was questioned about working conditions at New Lanark. These are some of his answers.

- The children work from six in the morning till seven at night, with half an hour at nine for breakfast and a whole hour for dinner.

- Teaching begins at seven-thirty in the evening and continues until nine o'clock. Besides the night schools there are two day schools for children too young to work.

- There are nearly 400 children who receive their food and clothing instead of a wage. They all live together in one house. There are six sleeping apartments for them, and three children are allowed to share one bed. Their summer clothes are made of cotton and they are washed once a fortnight. For a few months in summer both boys and girls go without shoes and stockings.

- They have oatmeal porridge for breakfast and supper, and sometimes there is milk with it. For dinner every day they have barley broth made from fresh beef. The beef itself is divided among one half of the children, about 200 g each. The other half of the children are given cheese so that they have either beef or cheese for dinner every day. Sometimes in winter they are given some herrings. They also have plenty of potatoes or coarse barley bread.

Robert Owen's ideas about the mill

In 1799 David Dale sold New Lanark to Robert Owen, his son-in-law. Under Owen's management New Lanark became famous as an example of a successful and profitable business where workers were treated much better than they were in mills elsewhere. He wanted to show that workers who were well-treated would work better than those who had to work in appalling conditions. Campaigners for factory reform visited New Lanark to learn more about Robert Owen's ideas. Children under the age of 10 were not allowed to work and the working hours of the older children were cut to 10 and three-quarter hours per day. At the same time, Owen provided reasonable housing for his workers. He also set up a village store which sold good quality products to the mill workers at cheaper prices than the other shops in the neighbourhood.

Source E

New Lanark in David Dale's time. Today the New Lanark Conservation Trust runs the village, which is now a World Heritage Site. Thousands of people from all over the world visit New Lanark each year.

Questions

1. There is no record of the questions David Dale was asked but his replies make it possible to guess what the questions were. Read each of his answers carefully and write down what you think the question may have been.

2. We know that conditions at New Lanark were better than the conditions in most other mills. What do David Dale's answers tell us about conditions in other mills at this time?

3. Look at Source E. Why do you think it is important to preserve New Lanark?

The Industrial Revolution 2 – what about the weavers?

Before the Industrial Revolution many men worked as handloom weavers, making yarn into cloth. Weavers often had a separate workshop attached to their homes to accommodate the loom. When the first spinning mills opened, more yarn was produced to be woven into cloth, and so handloom weavers were in great demand. Wages rose and men from Ireland and the Highlands moved to those areas of Scotland where there was a high demand for handloom weavers.

The good times

Weavers who earned good money had plenty of time to enjoy themselves. Many weavers were interested in politics and believed that the right to vote should be extended to working men like themselves. In Paisley, where there were large numbers of weavers, records show that they enjoyed sports such as golf, curling, fishing and hunting. There were also weavers's clubs where new ideas could be discussed.

━━ The bad times

By 1830, though, weavers had fallen on hard times. There were too many weavers looking for work and so employers paid low wages, knowing that if one weaver refused to work for the money offered, they could easily find someone else. In 1812 about 30,000 weavers went on strike, demanding that they be paid enough to keep themselves and their families. The employers, however, were against any kind of ruling about wages and some of the strike leaders were sent to prison for organising the strike. The campaign for a fair wage had failed.

Employers continued to pay low wages and the handloom weavers could do nothing to improve their conditions. After 1830 steam-powered mechanical looms, frequently operated by female factory workers, largely replaced the work of the handloom weavers. As a result, weavers who had once enjoyed considerable prosperity found themselves increasingly underpaid and then, with the invention of the power-driven looms, unemployed and living in great poverty.

Average weekly wages for Glasgow cotton weavers. (If these wages were converted into today's values, £1.00 per week would represent a reasonable weekly wage.)			
1810–16	£1.03	1821–25	£0.53
1816–20	£0.58	1826–30	£0.37
Numbers of handloom weavers in Scotland:			
1780	25,000	1820	78,000

Source F

◀ *A power-loom factory in 1850. This early photo shows the effect that factory looms had on the employment of handloom weavers.*

What were the long-term effects of the textile revolution?

The new towns

Steam-powered machinery meant that mills were no longer built beside rivers. New mills opened in existing towns which were near to the supplies of coal needed for the steam-powered machinery. Elsewhere new towns grew up round existing mills, to house the workers who came in from the country and the Highlands hoping for good wages and a better life. Barrhead, in East Renfrew, grew from a village of 30 families into a town with six mills and two weaving factories. Where there had previously been just one pub there were now 30.

Towns grew rapidly as houses were hastily built for the newly arrived workers. Landlords built cheap houses or split up older houses, so that many families lived in a single room. The combination of very long working hours, low wages and overcrowded rooms meant that, for many workers, life probably got worse, rather than better, in the first part of the nineteenth century.

Working conditions

During the early years of the Industrial Revolution there were no laws to protect the interests of the workers. Many people accepted that the employer had the right to do what he liked in his own factory, just as landlords did what they liked on their own land; there were no regulations about working conditions. Factory owners argued that workers were free to leave if they did not like the work. Gradually, however, after about 1830, this attitude changed, partly as a result of campaigns organised by factory workers and partly as a result of the efforts of middle-class reformers, who were horrified by the working conditions they saw in the mills.

In 1833 Parliament passed a law which said that children under the age of nine were not allowed to work in textile factories, while those under 13 could not work more than 48 hours a week. These changes did not go far enough to improve working conditions, but it was a start. Perhaps the most important aspect of this law was the fact that Parliament was prepared to pass laws which would provide some protection for the workers – although only for young children at this time.

37

Questions

1. Why were handloom weavers worse off in 1830 than they had been in 1815? You should try to mention at least three different reasons.

2. **a.** From the information you have read, describe four long-term effects of the textile revolution.

   b. Which do you think was the most important? Write a few sentences to explain your answer.

9 Changes in farming and travel

Was there an agricultural revolution?

> ❝In East Lothian we saw such large cornfields,
> such great fields of turnips and such stacks of hay as were
> surely never before seen anywhere on earth!❞
>
> *William Cobbett, an Englishman who toured Scotland in 1833.*

Farming in the 1830s was very different from farming in the early eighteenth century, when visitors commented on the backwardness of Scottish farming. At that time the land had been divided into narrow strips, or *runrigs*, and crops were grown every year on the most fertile ground so that the goodness of the soil was exhausted. Also, as there were no hedges or walls to separate the rigs, animals could easily damage the crops. Oats and barley were the main crops and there was nothing to feed to livestock in winter, so most cattle and sheep were killed in the autumn. Those that were kept through the winter were very weak and thin by the time that spring arrived. Much of the low-lying land was too wet to farm so potentially fertile land was wasted. Those who farmed the land could only just grow enough to keep themselves and their families and, in bad years, they might starve. Since many farmers only rented land for a few years at a time they had little reason to try to improve the land.

The need for change

The first people to introduce new farming ideas into Scotland were wealthy landowners who had learnt about changes taking place in England and in Holland. As the number of people living in towns increased with the growth of the factories, there was also an increase in the demand for food. This made it more worthwhile for farmers to improve their land.

What were these changes?

- Several rigs were combined and 'enclosed' with a hedge or wall to make larger fields.
- Large numbers of trees were planted.
- Drains were constructed so that surplus water could run off the land.
- Lime was added to the soil to fertilise it.
- New crops such as turnips and clover were grown as cattle fodder. More wheat was also planted.
- Careful breeding produced larger and stronger animals.
- A new, lighter plough made it easier to cultivate the land.
- Tenant farmers were able to rent their farms for longer periods – but they had to pay more rent each year.

These wealthy landowners spent a great deal of money on 'improving' their estates. At the same time they persuaded – or forced – some of the tenant farmers who rented land from them to introduce the new farming methods. Those tenants who would not change, or who could not afford the new, higher rents that the 'improving' landowners demanded, were often evicted from their farms.

How did the agricultural revolution affect ordinary people?

Source A

The present farmer has evicted seven or eight tenants in order to make his own farm bigger. Having been turned out of their homes, these poor families had no option but to send their children to work in the factories.

A visitor to Clydesdale in 1792.

Source B

In 1760 ploughmen earned £3.00 a year. Now in 1790, they can earn £8.00, or even £10.00 a year. In 1760 there was only one eight-day clock in the parish, six watches and one tea kettle. In 1790, there are 30 clocks, more than 100 watches and at least 160 tea kettles. Almost every family has at least one kettle and there are many that have two.

The Old Statistical Account for Fintry, 1790.

Source C

Despite the changes, life remained hard for those who lived and worked in the countryside. This photo was taken around 1900. ▶

39

Questions

1. List each of the changes in farming mentioned and state the advantages of each. Show your answers as a table, if you wish.

2. Sources A and B suggest that the agricultural revolution affected people in different ways. Use the sources to explain:
   a. why some people benefited
   b. why some people lost out.

3. How useful are photographs such as Source C as evidence of work in the countryside after the agricultural revolution?

How much did transport change between 1760 and 1830?

Travelling into the Highlands

In 1803 Elizabeth Grant travelled from Edinburgh to her home near Aviemore. Many years later she wrote down what she remembered of the journey. It took three days to travel a distance which can nowadays be driven in less than three hours. The Grants were wealthy and they had their own carriage but even so the journey was uncomfortable and tiring. First they had to cross the Firth of Forth, then the coach had to be put on a sailing boat and the journey across the Forth could last from one to three hours. On the third day of travelling, the coach approached the Grant's home but that was not the end of their journey (see Source D).

Source D

There was no good ford near the house. After a good view of our dear home, we had to drive on another two or three miles towards Aviemore. Then we turned off down a little used road through the birch woods to a ford, where there was a boat which could transport a carriage across the river. Once over the river, we were at home in Rothiemurchus.

Elizabeth Grant's account of her journey from Edinburgh to her home near Aviemore in 1803.

40

First-hand accounts such as the one in Source D make it clear that travelling by road was not easy at the beginning of the nineteenth century. It was, however, better than it had been 100 years earlier. Between about 1760 and 1830 many miles of new roads were built and new bridges made travelling easier – even though Elizabeth Grant's example makes it clear that there were still many areas where people had to be ferried across rivers by boat. Also, the work of engineers like Thomas Telford and John Macadam had improved the surface of roads so that it was less likely that carts and carriages would get stuck in deep ruts. In 1754 it took 10 days to travel by coach from Edinburgh to London, travelling at an average speed of just 6 km an hour. Thirty years later the same journey could be completed in 60 hours (two and a half days). Stage coaches and, later, mail coaches carried fare-paying passengers.

Easier travel by water

Changes in industry and in agriculture meant that there was a demand for cheap, efficient ways of getting raw materials and goods from one place to another. Water transport was one solution. Although roads were improving slowly, it was much easier to transport heavy and bulky goods by water. The River Clyde was dredged (dug out) to make it deeper so that ships could sail right up to Glasgow.

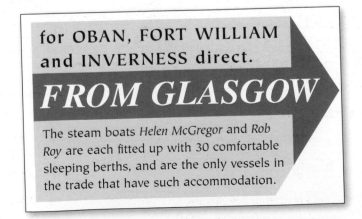

for OBAN, FORT WILLIAM and INVERNESS direct.

FROM GLASGOW

The steam boats *Helen McGregor* and *Rob Roy* are each fitted up with 30 comfortable sleeping berths, and are the only vessels in the trade that have such accommodation.

From an advertisement in the Glasgow Courier, 1835.

Canals were built and by 1822 the Forth–Clyde Canal and the Union Canal joined Edinburgh and Glasgow. Horse-drawn canal barges transported heavy loads, such as coal, and passengers travelled more comfortably by canal than they did by road. Although horses continued to pull the canal barges, there were also experiments with steam power. In 1812 the *Comet* (see Source F) started to carry passengers between Glasgow and Greenock, the first regular steamboat passenger service in Europe. It was soon possible to travel by steamboat from Glasgow to Fort William, and then along the Caledonian Canal to Inverness.

Source E

▲ *An early nineteenth-century view of Glasgow, showing a number of different ways of transporting people and goods.*

Source F

◀ *The* Comet *made use of both wind and steam power.*

Questions

1. Describe some of the ways in which goods were transported around Scotland in 1830.

2. Which of these methods of transport was not available in 1760?

3. Look carefully at Source E. Make a list of all of the ways in which horses and different types of boats are being used for transport.

4. Why did changes in industry and agriculture lead to improvements in transport?

10 *Life in the Highlands before 1800*

During most of the eighteenth century, few people travelled as far as the Highlands or the islands off the west coast of Scotland. Those who did were often shocked by the poverty they saw. As a result their evidence about Highland life can be one-sided.

Source A

▲ *Picture of the interior of a house on Islay, drawn in 1772.*

Source B

Their houses consist of a butt, a ben and a byre [a kitchen, an inner room and a place to keep cattle]. There is a fire by the wall but nothing like a chimney, only a hole in the roof so the whole wall is covered with soot. The earth floor is full of holes, retaining whatever wet or dirt may be thrown upon it. In one corner there is a box with a door in front. Inside the box there is a bed with a great many blankets. Into this box creep as many as it can hold, and thus they sleep, boxed in on every side, except the small door at the front.

A visitor to the Highlands in 1799 describes conditions inside a Highland house.

— Life in the valley of Strathnaver around 1800

One way of learning about the traditional Highland way of life is from the work of archaeologists. Excavations carried out at Rossal in the Strathnaver valley give us a clearer picture of what life was like for many people in the north of Scotland at the end of the eighteenth century.

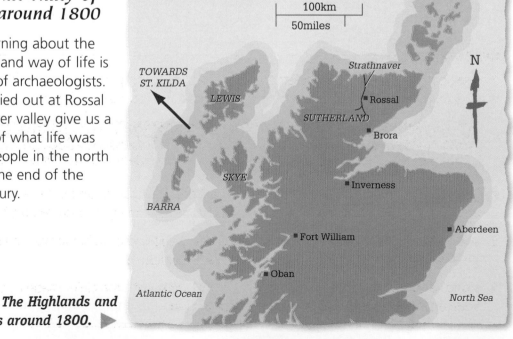

The Highlands and Islands around 1800. ▶

42

Today Strathnaver is a largely deserted valley in Sutherland. In 1800, however, there were about 12 townships, or small communities, in the valley. In Rossal there were 13 families, each living in a house built of peat blocks laid on stone foundations and with a roof made of peat and thatch. Timber was in short supply as very few large trees grew so far north. Roof timbers were often dug out of the deepest layers of the peat bogs on the moors, where the remains of ancient forests had been preserved in the peat.

Townships were surrounded by a wall. Inside the walled area was the *inbye*. Each family had a share of this better land on which they grew crops such as kail (cabbage), oats and bere (barley). In addition, potatoes were grown in special, raised beds, known as lazy beds, where soil, manure and seaweed helped to improve what was otherwise poor land. Sheep, which were small and delicate, were tethered and allowed to graze in the inbye. During the summer months cattle grazed on the shared *outbye*, or less fertile land, further away from the township.

Crops did not ripen properly in the short summers, so each family had a kiln in which the oats and bere were dried over a slow fire. During the long winter, the families lived off the food that they had stored in the summer and autumn. Salted meat and fish were rare luxuries. Occasionally one of the chickens that roosted in the rafters was killed and eaten. Mostly, though, the family lived on the dried grain which was kept in a wooden chest in the house, as well as potatoes and possibly turnips, which were protected from frost in specially dug pits in the byres (barns).

Source C

The people in Strathnaver lived happily. They didn't lack anything.

Angus Mackay, who lived in Strathnaver until he was 11, writing about the years immediately before 1814.

43

Questions

1. Use Sources A and B to complete the following table, comparing all the evidence provided in each of the two sources. The first example has been completed for you.

	Source A	Source B
Evidence	Open fire with no chimney	Mentions that there is no chimney

2. Use your completed table to answer the question: 'How far do Sources A and B agree about conditions inside Highland homes at the end of the eighteenth century?'

3. The artist who drew Source A wrote very critically about the Highland way of life. Do you think that this means that Source A is unreliable evidence?

4. Using all of the evidence in this section, do you agree with the claim made by the author of Source C? You should give reasons for your answer.

— Changes in the Highland way of life

Highland society was changing throughout the eighteenth century and these changes accelerated after 1745, when the government tried to destroy the old Highland way of life in the years after the Jacobites were defeated at the Battle of Culloden (see page 18). Other reasons for changes to Highland society were:

- Some chiefs were impressed by the wealth of landowners in the Lowlands of Scotland and wanted a similar lifestyle themselves. To do this they needed to increase the amount of rent they received from the tenants on their land. Some believed that if they increased the income from their land they could carry out improvements, just as landowners further south were doing. They hoped that in time these changes would also improve their tenants's standard of living.

- The number of people living in the Highlands was growing rapidly. People were better fed because potatoes, which were introduced into the Highlands in the 1740s, ensured that people did not starve, even if their diet was very dull. This population growth created new problems because traditional farming could not provide enough food for all of the people living on the land.

- There was a growing demand in the rest of Britain for Highland products such as cattle, wool, kelp (an alkali produced from seaweed which was used in the manufacture of soap and glass) and fish.

— What were the Highland Clearances?

In order to increase their wealth and carry out improvements, Highland landlords started to create larger farms for which they could charge higher rents. To do this they often forced the inhabitants of the traditional townships off their land. This development was known as the Highland Clearances. In many cases these larger farms were let to men who introduced new breeds of sheep to graze on the hills and in the valleys. These new tenant farmers could afford the higher rents because they could get a good price for the sale of their wool.

Income from rent paid in Glengarry	
1768	£732
1802	£4184

— Where did the traditional farmers go?

For those who had been evicted from the townships there was little choice. They did not just lose their homes; they also lost the traditional grazing grounds for their cattle, so had to give up their animals and lose their source of income.

- Many were encouraged to move to the coast, where they rented a small croft and found a part-time job such as fishing or working in the kelp industry. This additional income was vital as the croft was too small to support the family.

- Some felt that they had no option but to leave Scotland and start a new life overseas.

- Many ended up heading for the growing towns of the Lowlands, to seek work as weavers or factory workers.

- Others joined the Highland regiments to fight in Britain's wars overseas.

44

Source D

The great majority of Highlanders were tenants and under Scottish law they had no legal rights to the land they farmed. Highland landlords were allowed almost complete freedom of action to do what they wanted without any interference from the government.

A modern historian writing in 1985. He believes that Scottish tenants could be evicted more easily than in many other parts of Europe.

Many Highlanders moved to the coast where they lived in crofting communities like the one shown here, near Stornoway in 1900. With so little land to farm, people depended on potatoes which produced more food per acre than other crops. When the potato harvest failed in the 1840s, whole crofting communities faced starvation. ▼

Source E

Questions

1. Make a list of reasons to explain why so many Highlanders faced eviction between 1790 and 1830. Which do you think was the most significant reason? Explain your answer.

2. The table of income from rent paid in Glengarry and Source D help us understand why the Highland Clearances took place.

   a. What is suggested by the table on page 44?

   b. What is suggested by Source D?

3. 'Few people seemed to care what happened to the ordinary people of the Highlands.'

   Using the evidence in the table and the sources, and your own knowledge, write a paragraph explaining how far you agree with this statement.

What happened at Rossal? A study of the clearances in Strathnaver

Most of Sutherland belonged to Elizabeth, Countess of Sutherland. When she and her husband, the Earl of Stafford, wanted to modernise the running of the Sutherland estates they employed well paid advisors. Having decided that much of the interior of Sutherland was best suited to sheep farming, they were prepared to invest large sums of money in developing new industries on the coast. New fishing villages were built at Helmsdale and Bettyhill and a coal mine was opened at Brora, to provide work and to bring industry to the area.

Two men were appointed to carry out the work. In 1813 they decided to clear Strathnaver and introduce sheep farms into the area. Patrick Sellar, who intended to rent one of these sheep farms, was responsible for organising the clearance.

The events which followed are still controversial. Sellar wanted to clear the tenants off the land as quickly as possible, although it was known that many of those who were to be cleared would have nowhere else to go. In June 1814 Sellar moved in with men and dogs to help him clear the valley. Houses were pulled down and burned. Rossal – the township which archaeologists have excavated (see Source H) – was among those destroyed in this way. In 1816 Patrick Sellar was charged with arson and causing the death of two people but the jury found him innocent. The trial still gives rise to argument: was the verdict justified or was the jury biased towards Sellar? Sources F and G present two views on the Strathnaver Clearances.

Source F

I was present at the burning of the house of William Chisholm, in which was lying his wife's mother, an old bed-ridden woman of nearly 100 years of age. When Mr Sellar arrived I told him the old woman was not fit to be moved. He replied, 'Damn her, the old witch, she has lived too long – let her burn'. Fire was immediately set to the house, and the blankets in which she was carried were in flames before she could be got out. She died within five days.

The cries of the women and the children, the roaring of the cattle, the smoke and fire, presented a scene that had to be seen to be believed. I climbed up a hill at about eleven o'clock in the evening and counted 250 blazing houses. The fire lasted six days till all the dwellings were reduced to ashes.

Twenty-five years after these events, Donald Macleod, who lived in Rossal and witnessed the clearance, wrote a book called Gloomy Memories *in which he described what he remembered.*

Source G

The people who were to be removed were to hold their farms rent free for the last year on condition that they would move to their new crofts without delay. Some of the people, however, reappeared and constructed new huts, or repaired their old turf huts and reoccupied their former possessions. This made it necessary to evict them a second time. To prevent the possibility of a repetition the only course was to burn the timber. Those accounts which claim that this was done with cruelty or oppression are absolutely wrong.

James Loch, an estate manager for the Countess of Sutherland.

46

Source H

▲ *All that remains of the township of Rossal today. Before the 1814 clearance it was a self-sufficient farming community. The remains of many such communities can be seen throughout the Highlands.*

Questions

1. Describe what happened in Strathnaver in 1814. In your answer, mention the plans of the Countess of Sutherland as well as the events of 1814.

2. Read Sources F and G about the Strathnaver Clearances.

   a. Make a list of the ways in which the two sources agree.

   b. Make a list of the ways in which the two sources disagree.

   c. Explain why the two sources differ so much about the clearances in Strathnaver.

3. Why do people still disagree about the clearances in Strathnaver, almost 200 years later?

11

The French Revolution

In July 1789 astonishing news reached Scotland. The people of Paris had stormed the Bastille – the royal prison located in the heart of Paris – and murdered the prison governor. Visitors to Paris saw the crowds parading through the streets with the governor's head displayed on a soldier's pike while others started to demolish the prison itself (see Source A).

This event marked the start of the French Revolution. While revolutions in industry and agriculture were taking place throughout Scotland, across the Channel in France people had begun to question the way in which the country was governed. The Bastille symbolised royal power in France and the events of 14 July 1789 were a revolutionary challenge to the authority of the King. In 1789 ordinary French men and women rebelled because they wanted 'liberty' and 'equality'. Many people in Britain greeted the news of these events with great enthusiasm. At first there was little sympathy for the French king, who was criticised for being too powerful. Some went further and hoped that the debate about liberty and equality in France would bring about changes in Britain too.

 Source A

▲ *Houel's painting of the storming of the Bastille in Paris, July 1789.*

Many Scots felt that they had good reason to welcome the events of 1789. King George III was not as powerful as the French king because he had to work with Parliament; however, very few people in Scotland had the right to vote in parliamentary elections. There were just 33 men in Edinburgh who had the right to vote for the MP who would represent the city in the House of Commons in Westminster, London. There were also so few voters throughout the whole of the country that for the last 20 years of the eighteenth century it was possible for one man – Sir Henry Dundas – to use bribery and corruption to make sure that only his supporters were elected to the House of Commons. Dundas was a landowner and a successful lawyer who used his own position in the government to offer a huge range of well-paid jobs to those who promised him their support. It seemed that, unofficially, Dundas ruled Scotland; he was nicknamed 'Harry the Ninth, the uncrowned King of Scotland'.

The French Revolution and Napoleon

Before 1789 the French king was an 'absolute monarch', which meant that there were no restrictions on what decisions he could make or how he governed the country. Although the nobility and some members of the Catholic Church were very wealthy and enjoyed great privileges, the majority of French people were very poor and had few rights.

As a result of events in the summer of 1789 the French king, Louis XVI, was forced to make changes in the way that France was governed. The special privileges of the nobility and clergy were abolished, and there was talk of all people being equal and of there being freedom from the traditional restrictions and duties for the peasants and working classes. However, Louis was reluctant to accept the changes and few people trusted him after he and his wife tried to escape from Paris. In 1793 he was found guilty of plotting against the country and sentenced to death by guillotine (a machine for beheading people in which a metal blade fell from a height down two vertical guides).

The death of Louis XVI did not end France's troubles and for the next two years an emergency government executed almost anyone who dared to criticise it. There were almost daily executions and people talked of a 'Reign of Terror'. During this time Paris workers debated politics eagerly and demanded further changes. To show their support for the revolution they often wore a red cap, known as the 'cap of liberty', a symbol which came to arouse real fear among those who opposed the revolution.

To make matters worse, many countries declared war on France in an attempt stop the revolutionary ideas from spreading. Although the period of terror ended in 1795, the foreign wars continued. A young army general, Napoleon Bonaparte, achieved great military success for France and seized power in 1799; by 1804 he had declared himself Emperor of the French. Napoleon was determined to dominate Europe and until 1815, when he was defeated at the Battle of Waterloo, the fear of 'Boney' united the people of Britain. Between 1793 and 1815 many Scots were enlisted to fight overseas against the French and their allies.

49

Examples of what might have made the news headlines in 1792. Although the events these newsflashes describe are presented in a modern style, all of these incidents actually took place. ▼

The people protest!
Straw guys of Dundas burnt in
Aberdeen, Brechin, Perth and Dundee!

Three nights of riots in Edinburgh! Stone throwers have attacked the home of Sir Henry Dundas!

In some villages and towns, the people have copied the French and put up so-called Trees of Liberty! Some have even put on the red 'cap of liberty' worn by the extreme revolutionaries in France!

The revolutionary government in France has promised support to revolutionaries in other countries!

'No more Lords or Dukes,' says Paine. 'Every man should have the vote!' The government has now banned Tom Paine's book *The Rights of Man* but hundreds of copies have been sold in Scotland!

50

A young lawyer, Thomas Muir, has been found guilty of organising the Society of the Friends of the People. His crime? He wants all men to have the right to vote! His punishment? Transportation to Australia. *Let the people of Scotland remember him as a martyr!*

Weapons dump found in Edinburgh! Robert Watt, a tailor, has been found guilty and hanged outside the Tolbooth! His head is cut off and shown to the people to remind them of what happens to traitors!

Questions

1. Read through the 'newsflashes' carefully. Make a list of all of the evidence that you can find to support the view, 'The people of Scotland were influenced by the revolutionaries in France.'

2. Make a list of all of the evidence that you can find to support the view, 'In the 1790s the British government was frightened that there might be a revolution in Scotland.'

3. After 1799, the fear of revolution disappeared until after 1815. Can you think of any reasons to explain why this happened?

Was there a threat of revolution after 1815?

In the years after 1815 there were further protests in Scotland. Economic problems and rising unemployment made workers aware of how little power they had to alter government policies. In 1816 discontented weavers helped organise large public meetings in Paisley and Glasgow to draw attention to their problems. There were also demands that all adult men should be given the right to vote in parliamentary elections and that MPs should be paid, so that any man could afford to stand for election to parliament. Once again, many of the protesters put on the 'cap of liberty'.

By early 1817 it was known that secret societies had been established to try to bring about far-reaching changes, and there was also talk of threats to overthrow the government. There were rumours that the members of these societies were armed. Alarmed by similar demonstrations in England, in 1819 the government introduced new repressive laws which forbade people to hold meetings involving more than 50 people. Those who most wanted change – the Radicals – now set up a central planning committee and increased their contact with Radicals in the north of England.

Who were the Radicals?

The Radicals were men who wanted far-reaching changes in the way that Britain was governed. They demanded the following changes:

- a vote for every adult man
- frequent elections so that governments would have to carry out reforms quickly if they wanted to be re-elected
- payment for MPs.

Some Radicals wanted to overthrow the government by force but many accepted that changes needed to be introduced peacefully.

What did the Radicals do?

On 1 April 1820 the Radicals distributed a pamphlet titled 'Address to the Inhabitants of Great Britain and Ireland' which was published, it was claimed, by a committee responsible for forming a provisional temporary government. This title suggested the Radicals planned to overthrow the existing government. Was Britain really on the verge of revolution? The government seemed to think that the threat was real. The Address called on workers to go on strike and reports claimed that 60,000 workers were already out on strike.

However, the general uprising that was promised did not take place. Instead a group of about twenty Scottish Radicals, most of whom were weavers, decided to march from Glasgow to the Carron Ironworks in Falkirk, to seize some of the cannon made there (see map on page 33). In fact, they never reached Falkirk. Mounted soldiers stopped them at Bonnymuir and 18 of them were taken prisoner. Further west, at Strathaven, another 100 Radicals marched towards Glasgow bearing a banner which proclaimed 'Scotland free or a desart'. (The Radicals meant 'desert' but clearly they were not well-educated and so spelt the word incorrectly.) However, by the time that the Strathaven marchers reached Rutherglen it was clear that the national uprising was not going to take place and the group quickly broke up. The strikers all returned to work and the 'revolution' did not take place.

Source B

All the weavers in Glasgow and its suburbs have struck work, and our streets are crowded with them walking about idle. The weavers in Paisley have also ceased to work and the miners round about have likewise come out on strike this morning.

About mid-day the Dunbartonshire Yeoman Cavalry arrived in town and in the afternoon the Ayrshire Yeoman Cavalry. More troops are expected in the course of the day. In some places strangers have taken possession of blacksmiths' shops and have started to make pikes. The times are extremely dangerous.

From the **Glasgow Courier,** *3 April 1820.*

Source C

Between 30 and 40 Radicals armed with guns, pistols, pikes etc., apparently from Glasgow, marched through the village of Cordorrat, about ten miles east from this city, in military order. They took two guns from people in the village.

From the **Glasgow Courier,** *4 April 1820.*

— *What was the significance of the events of 1820?*

The government was clearly alarmed by the threat of revolution. Even though it was very unlikely that the uprising could have succeeded, the events of April 1820 reinforced fears that the workers could not be trusted. It was only much later, in the nineteenth century, that some – although not all – working men were given the right to vote. Even then, it was almost another fifty years before all adult men were finally allowed to vote in parliamentary elections. Politicians proved even more reluctant to give women the right to vote: it was not until 1928 that women had the same voting rights as men.

Events between 1815 and 1820, and government attempts to silence protest meetings, convinced large numbers of working men that the whole system of government was corrupt and must be changed. Just as importantly, however, they realised that peaceful protests were more likely to succeed than violent ones. The events of 1820 therefore help to explain why those people who campaigned in nineteenth-century Scotland to extend the right to vote concentrated mainly on peaceful ways of trying to achieve change.

Questions

1. Write down at least three reasons which help to explain why some people were plotting against the government in 1820.

2. How useful is the extract from the *Glasgow Courier* (Source B) as evidence of events at the beginning of April 1820?

3. Read the newspaper extracts for 3 and 4 April (Sources B and C).

   Write an article for the *Glasgow Courier* for 6 April, the day after the so-called 'Battle of Bonnymuir' had taken place.

12

The Scots abroad

Scots had emigrated and started new lives overseas even before 1700, so by the end of the eighteenth century a considerable number had settled abroad, mainly in Britain's North American colonies. The nineteenth century, however, was to be a century of mass emigration from Europe. Historians estimate that between 1815 and 1914 about 44 million people left Europe to start new lives; among them were some two million Scots. Given that the total population of Scotland was relatively small, there were very few other countries from which such a large percentage of the total population emigrated. Only Ireland and Norway experienced a similarly high rate of emigration during this period.

Why did so many Scots leave?

The sources that follow each suggest at least one reason why so many Scots emigrated between 1700 and 1900. Some suggest that Scots were forced to leave (these reasons are called 'push factors') and others suggest that people were attracted by the prospects of a new life in another country (known as 'pull factors').

Source A

Over there a day labourer can earn three times the wages he can in this country. There are no beggars in America. There are no titles or proud lords to tyrannise over the lower sort of people, men being more upon the level.

*From the **Edinburgh Advertiser**, 1774.*

Source B

A very principal reason must be, that the people when turned out of their farms to make way for sheep, see no way to make a living in their country.

Thomas Telford, writing about Scottish emigration in the early nineteenth century.

Source C

The condition of the poor people all over the Highlands is fearful. We frequently have bad springs but this is the winter of starvation after one of the 'bad springs'.

The minister for Bracadale, on the Island of Skye, December 1846.

53

Source D

A REAL "SCOTTISH GRIEVANCE."

DUNCAN.—"Oh! but my mother is frail, and can't be sent out of the country in that ship; will you not let Flora and her ————."
FACTOR.—[sternly] "No, no lad—move on with the old woman; she will not be here in the way of his Lordship's sheep and deer."

◀ *An illustration from 'Real Scottish Grievances', a pamphlet published in 1854 describing evictions from the Macdonald estates in Skye.*

Source E

THE CALEDONIAN Voyage to MONEY-LAND.

▲ *A cartoon titled 'The Caledonian voyage to money land'. The cartoonist is suggesting that Scots emigrated because they wanted to make their fortune, and that he has little faith in such hopes.*

54

Source F

Any working man or woman, of whatever trade or calling, and especially the labouring class, can do far better here in Australia than at home, and with one half the trouble and care, too. I hope that many more of our Aberdeenshire folk will come out. They will do well.

A letter from Australia, published in the Aberdeenshire Journal, 1852.

Source G

In 1892 the Canadian government appointed two full-time agents in Scotland to promote emigration. They undertook a tour of markets, hiring fairs, agricultural shows and village halls. The illustrated lecture, using the magic lantern, was a favourite device. The agent for the north of Scotland was even able to deliver his presentation in Gaelic if the audience required it.

From a modern historian writing in 1999.

Source H

To create a sporting estate, Sir James Matheson, whose family's firm Jardine Matheson had made a fortune from the opium trade in China, cleared over 2000 tenants off Lewis. But he did provide transport, supplies and some financial aid for their journey to Canada. Gordon of Cluny, hoping to sell Barra to the government as a convict island, drove 1500 off his estate, whipping the more reluctant on to the boats.

Quoted by a modern historian writing in 1996 about the 1840–50s.

Questions

1. Study Sources A–H carefully. Copy this diagram into your notes and then use the information in the sources to complete it. The first line has been started for you.

Source	Primary (P) / Secondary (S)	Push factors	Pull factors
A	P		Better wages

2. When you have completed the table, use the information to provide a balanced answer to the question: 'How far do you agree with the view that Scots emigrated because they were forced to leave the country?'

The Scots in Australia

Over 200,000 Scots emigrated to Australia between 1788 and 1900, braving a journey which took about three months in 1850. Many of those who went were to make an important contribution to the development of the country.

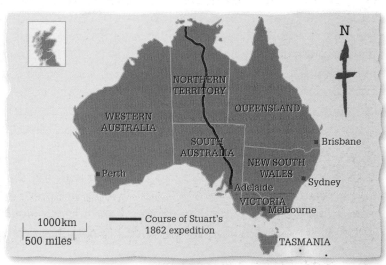

Map of Australia showing relative size of Scotland. ▲

Although many of Australia's earliest settlers were men and women convicted of crimes in Britain, relatively few Scots were sentenced to transportation to Botany Bay in Australia. English criminals outnumbered the Scots by about four to one. Among those Scots who were sent to Australia, however, was Thomas Muir, who had dared to openly criticise the government during the 1790s (see page 50), and 19 of the leaders of the so-called 'Radical war' of 1820 (see pages 51–2). Thomas Watling, from Dumfries, was transported for forging banknotes. Once he was in Australia, he put his artistic skills to good use and his watercolour paintings of Aboriginal (native) life are an important historical record (see Source J).

(see page 50), ... (see pages 51–2). ... (see Source J).

Source I

A linen scarf produced in Scotland to commemorate the trial of Thomas Muir and those who were sentenced to transportation to Australia with him. ▶

55

Source J

◀ Aboriginals going to a meeting with the governor, 1790, by Thomas Watling.

Were Scots involved in the exploration of Australia?

Because much of central Australia consists of desert, it was not explored for many years. By the 1840s, however, various attempts were made to find out more about the interior of the country. John McDouall Stuart, who had emigrated to New South Wales on the south-east coast of Australia in 1839, was invited to join an exploratory expedition in 1844. Conditions were terrible: temperatures of 55°C were recorded in the shade and the extreme heat burned the skin of their dog's feet! When he returned, Stuart was determined that one day he would cross the continent.

Twice he failed but a third expedition set off from Adelaide on the south coast in December 1861. This time Stuart succeeded in reaching the Indian Ocean, in the north of Australia (see map on page 55). Just over a year after he had set off, Stuart returned to Adelaide. Coughing up blood and near to death, he was carried the last 1126 km (700 miles) on a stretcher slung between four horses.

Factfile – the Scots in Australia

- The cost of travelling to Australia meant that the early settlers had to be reasonably well off to be able to afford the journey. After 1837, however, subsidies (grants of money from the government) were available for the voyage out. In 1836 only 136 Scots had emigrated to Australia; in 1838, 3215 emigrated.

- In 1852, 36 islanders from St Kilda, a tiny, remote island off the west coast of Scotland, set off for Australia. They represented a third of the total population of the island. Sixteen of them died of fever during the long, unhealthy voyage.

- The discovery of gold in the 1850s attracted many Scots to Australia.

- It was not just Scots from the Highlands and Islands who went to Australia.

Many left Scotland's cities to find work as labourers and servants in Australia's rapidly growing towns.

- Scots played an important part in establishing schools, hospitals, churches, banks and libraries in Australia. They were also successful businessmen. One visitor observed: 'Those who make money are generally Scotsmen'.

- Many people occupied land as squatters, often forcing the Aboriginal people off their land. These squatters set up sheep farms, producing wool which was exported back to Britain. A squatter's life could be harsh and lonely, but some were very successful and established large and profitable sheep farms.

Extension task

1. 'Scots made a big contribution overseas.'

Investigate the contribution made by Scots to the development of either the USA or Canada or Australia.

You will need to:

a. plan your investigation

b. identify several different sources of information

c. select relevant information

d. present your findings

e. reach a balanced conclusion.

13 'Going for a soldier'

Many Scots left Scotland for long periods of time to serve with the British army overseas. In the 200 years after the Act of Union, Scottish soldiers fought in Europe as well as in America, India and Africa. Even during peacetime, Scottish regiments spent many years overseas, policing and protecting Britain's expanding Empire.

Source A

I should imagine that two or three independent Highland companies might be of use in Canada. They are hardy, intrepid, accustomed to rough country, and it is no great loss if they fall.

General Wolfe, who led the successful attack against the French in Canada in 1759.

For most of the years between 1793 and 1815 Britain was at war with France (see page 49). New regiments were raised in Scotland and Scots found themselves fighting not only in Europe but even as far away as India. Many recruits were forced to join up, only to find that army life was extremely harsh and poorly paid. Soldiers received 5p a day, but after payment for food and uniform was deducted this left the soldier with about 8p a week as spending money. The daily food ration was often inadequate (see Source C) and soldiers were expected to seize any additional food that they could find from the local people. As a result, it was not surprising that the soldiers were on occasion undisciplined (see Source D).

Source B

VOLUNTEERS WANTED

For General FRASER's Highland Regiment

These soldiers are to go to America to put down the present American Rebellion.

Considering that the British army will be from 40–50,000 strong, the rebellion will be entirely put down by next summer. Then you will get your reward. The land of the rebels will be divided amongst you and everyone of you will become lairds. Is this not better than starving at home in these poor times?

Any of you who has got a cross wife, or smarts under the displeasure of an unloving parent, come and join up!

A recruitment poster, dated January 1776.

Source D

When the town surrendered, the gates were opened and we were allowed to enter the town with the purpose of plundering it. Each man ran in the direction that pleased him, bursting open doors and rummaging through the houses, breaking up the most valuable items of furniture. Many men went immediately to the spirit stores, where, having drunk a great deal, they were prepared for every sort of mischief.

The writer is describing what happened when a Scottish regiment took the town of Badajoz in Spain, in 1812.

Source C

We had to depend on our daily allowance of one pound (400 g) of hard biscuit, one pound of beef and one third of a pint of spirits. The biscuit was frequently crushed to crumbs, or mouldered to dust, and the beef would not have been allowed a stall in the poorest market of Great Britain.

A Scottish soldier in Spain in 1813.

After 1815, Scottish soldiers were frequently posted to distant parts of the British Empire where they had to deal with rebellions and local uprisings, which were often protests against British rule. Scottish regiments fought on the north-west frontier in India, as well as in Afghanistan. They saw action, too, in South Africa and in Egypt. Scottish soldiers were widely admired both for their bravery in battle and for their loyal contribution to the defence of the Empire.

Almost everywhere, conditions were harsh and the risk of dying from disease was considerable. For most Scots, however, no destination could have seemed much more remote than serving with the British army in India. In central India the heat and dust were overwhelming and the men spent much of the day restricted to barracks, able to work only in the early morning and in the evening. Rats and snakes were commonplace around the barracks and drinking water was often contaminated, causing cholera and fever.

Source E

We marched back to Madras and camped there for a short time, then marched up the country to Trichinopoly. That must be the hottest place in the east, it is quite possible to lay a piece of beef on a stone, any time from eight o'clock in the morning till four pm, and it will be ready for eating directly. It is so hot, the men say that there is only a sheet of foolscap paper between it and the other place (i.e. hell). We then marched to the Nilgiri hills, which are 2438 metres above sea level. It was very cold up there but I liked it well. I used to keep some poultry, such as cocks and hens. The soldiers lived in mud huts but they are building a fine barracks there. Believe me that Arthur's Seat in Edinburgh is nothing to the Nilgiris.

From a letter sent home to Glasgow from India, 1855.

Source F

◀ *Highland soldiers captured the popular imagination during the occupation of Paris after the battle of Waterloo, 1815–8.*

Questions

1. Explain why General Wolfe (Source A) believed that Highland soldiers would be useful in Canada. What does this reveal about attitudes towards Highlanders at that time?

2. Why did so many Scots join the army, despite the poor conditions?
You should consider the prospects for men in Scotland as well as the possible attractions of life in the army.

14 The 'railway revolution'

Canals and stage coaches had improved transport considerably between the 1760s and 1830s, but the real revolution in transport came with the building of the railways. Within 20 years of the opening of the first passenger service in Scotland, almost all of the major cities were linked by rail.

The first 'railways' were railroads for horse-drawn wagons. The rails reduced friction, making it easier for the horses to pull heavy loads. By 1824 there were over 145 km (90 miles) of these railroads, often taking coal from the pithead to a harbour, or to industries needing large supplies of coal.

In 1831 steam locomotives were used for the first time between Garnkirk (on the Monklands coalfield) and St Rollox Station in Glasgow (see Source A). Just over 10 years later, in 1842, the line between Edinburgh and Glasgow was opened by Queen Victoria. Within three years, nearly 1.9 million passengers had used this line. Rail passenger travel grew rapidly during the 1840s as more and more towns and cities were linked to either Edinburgh or Glasgow. By 1850 – less than 20 years after the opening of the Garnkirk to Glasgow line – there were about 1000 miles (1600 km) of railways in Scotland, and both Glasgow and Edinburgh had direct rail links with London.

Rail transport revolutionised trade. Fresh food could be transported quickly and cheaply to the cities; goods which were manufactured in one part of the country were now sold all over the country, rather than just locally. At the same time, improvements in both locomotives and carriages meant that rail travel was faster and more comfortable than any other form of passenger transport.

Source A

▲ *The opening of the Glasgow–Garnkirk railway in 1831.*

Source B

A steam engine on the Glasgow to Edinburgh line in 1831 pulling a variety of carriages. ▲

Source C

At present goods are carried from Edinburgh to Glasgow by canal, or by carts and wagons on the public road, at an expense varying from 80p to £2.00 per ton, and taking from eighteen hours to four days. Using the proposed railway the merchant and manufacturer will save money in the carriage of their goods, and the householder will get cheap coal. The professional man and the tourist will get a cheap and speedy means of conveyance and the landholder will find an extensive market for his mineral and agricultural produce.

From a report published in 1831 explaining the benefits of the proposed railway between Edinburgh and Glasgow.

Source D

Sale of Horses!

To be sold at Mr Wordsworth's this day at one o'clock excellent harness horses, which have been working in the Edinburgh and Glasgow coaches, and are withdrawn, in consequence of the Opening of the Edinburgh and Glasgow Railway. These horses are very powerful, and will be found useful for farm work.

From an advertisement in **The Scotsman,** *9 March 1842.*

Questions

1. Look carefully at the carriages illustrated in Source B. Each carriage suggests a possible use for the railway. What does each carriage tell us about these uses?

2. What are the advantages of the proposed railway, according to Source C?

3. Produce a publicity brochure for the Edinburgh–Glasgow Railway Company.

   a. You should point out the advantages of this line.

   b. You must appeal to all the people who will use the railway as well as those who may want to invest some money in the company.

   c. Remember to use a big headline to catch people's attention.

   d. Use the Internet, if available, for information and to download any contemporary illustrations into your finished work.

Workshop of the world

In 1888 over 5.7 million people visited the Glasgow International Exhibition, the first of three highly successful international exhibitions organised to publicise the city's success as a centre of industry and manufacturing. The exhibition was held in Kelvingrove Park, and a vast cream and red timber building, decorated with minarets and domes, was constructed to house it. Entrance tickets cost one shilling (5p) and the displays inside acted as a 'shop-window' for industry. In the Machinery Court industrialists could inspect the latest machines while an illuminated 'Fairy Fountain' demonstrated the potential of electricity. Elsewhere an Indian bazaar emphasised the importance of trade with the Empire.

The building was quickly named 'Baghdad by Kelvinside' but its exotic appearance succeeded in drawing attention to the achievements of the city. Glasgow was now known as the 'Second City of the Empire' because it had made such an important contribution to Britain's position as the 'workshop of the world'.

Iron and steel, engineering and ship building

The Industrial Revolution had started with rapid changes in the production of textiles, but by the 1830s dramatic changes in other industries were transforming Scotland's economy and, with it, Scottish society. Coal mining, iron and steel production, engineering and shipbuilding were expanding rapidly, as the tables below show.

Source A

By 1913 one relatively small geographical area of Scotland – Glasgow, and the nearby towns in the west of Scotland – made one fifth of the steel and one third of the ships produced in the whole of the United Kingdom. In addition, they built half of all British-made ships' engines and one third of railway engines, carriages and trucks.

A modern historian writing in 1986.

Scottish coal production (in million tons)	
1800	2.0
1854	7.4
1860	10.9
1913	42.5

Number of iron furnaces in Scotland	
1830	27
1840	70
1850	143
1860	171

Scottish iron output (in tons)	
1806	22,000
1830	37,000
1840	241,000
1852	775,000
1860	1,017,000

Percentage of steel-built ships produced on the Clyde	
1879	10
1889	97.3

The iron industry required coal for its furnaces and so the output of Scotland's coal mines also increased. The growing rail network made it possible to transport the coal while Irish immigrants, newly arrived in Scotland, provided much of the workforce needed to extract the coal. The rapid extension of the railways, in turn, demanded new and better locomotives, which put Scottish engineering expertise to good use. By the end of the nineteenth century locomotives manufactured in Scotland were so much in demand that they were being exported all over the world (see Source D).

Shipbuilding, too, was becoming a major industry. Scottish engineers were among the first to experiment with steam-powered ships and from this developed further pioneering work using iron, rather than wood, in ship construction. Clyde shipyards eventually started to use steel to build ships in order to remain as competitive as possible in world markets. 'Clyde built' was associated with high quality and the Clydeside shipyards were famous throughout the world.

Jute from Camperdown

Elsewhere in Scotland industries were also changing fast. In Dundee textiles continued to be important but jute (used in canvas and sacking) gradually replaced linen as the main raw material. Jute was so important in Dundee that the town became known as Juteopolis and the Camperdown Works in Lochee was the largest jute mill in the world. Camperdown's 14,000 workers were mainly women because they could be employed more cheaply than men. Like Glasgow, Dundee was heavily dependent on overseas trade. The jute was imported from India, manufactured and then re-exported throughout the world.

Source B

Wheat grown on the Canadian prairies had to be taken by rail to eastern ports, and the locomotive could well be made in Glasgow while the sacks holding the grain were quite likely to have been manufactured in Dundee. The ships that transported the grain across the North Atlantic were often built and engineered on the Clyde.

A modern historian writing in 1980.

Source C

Scotland was truly a force to be reckoned with in the world economy and had achieved a position of manufacturing supremacy out of all proportion to the small size of her population.

A modern historian writing in 1999.

Source D

▲ *Scottish-made locomotives were exported all over the world. This is a 1910 locomotive on the Calcutta–Darjeeling line in India.*

Questions

1. Read Sources A, B and C and the text in this section. Explain why Glasgow was described as the 'second city of the Empire' towards the end of the nineteenth century.

2. Design an advertising poster for the Glasgow International Exhibition of 1888. You might mention:

a. the location

b. the exhibition buildings

c. the main exhibits and attractions

d. the reasons why people should be proud of Scottish achievements.

Did industrialisation benefit the people of Scotland?

There were fortunes to be made from these industrial developments. A few, like the Paisley-based Coats brothers, became multi-millionaires, and there were others, like Sir William Burrell in Glasgow or the Dundee jute manufacturer Frederick Sharp, whose enormous wealth enabled them to become collectors of treasures purchased at home and abroad. The middle classes, too, prospered in the second half of the nineteenth century, often moving to handsome stone-built villas in the suburbs, well away from the noise and grime of the industrial areas.

The vast majority of the population, however, were not so fortunate. Wages were low and in many jobs workers were taken on only for very short periods of time. Unemployment was a constant threat and there was no financial help from the government for those who were out of work, or were too ill or old to be employed. As a result many people lived all of their lives in poverty.

Despite some efforts to reduce overcrowding in the city slums towards the end of the century, many families were still forced to live in tenement 'single ends' (see page 37), unable to afford anything else. The census of 1861 revealed that 64 per cent of the entire population lived in one- or two-roomed houses. In Glasgow in 1886 a third of all families were living in a single room which probably did not measure much more than 4.5 by 3.5 metres.

Cholera

With so many people living in such overcrowded conditions, it was not surprising that disease spread quickly. Well water was often contaminated and the lack of sewers and organised rubbish collections meant that human and household waste piled up. In 1832 there was a major outbreak of cholera, a water-borne disease, in which 10,000 Scots died.

Source E

In many one-room houses we saw no furniture at all and the whole family, including men, women and children, huddled together at night on such straw or rags as they can gather.

Glasgow housing report, 1886.

63

Source F

Dundee had only five water closets for a population of 92,000 in 1861, with three of those in hotels.

A modern historian writing in 1992.

Source G

Tea with sugar and bread without butter is very usual fare. Porridge and milk, broth and beef may be seen in a limited number of houses, but not where the poorest families live.

The main meal of the day in Glasgow in 1886.

Source H

▲ *The Saltmarket, Glasgow, in the 1860s, showing slum conditions.*

It was only when town councils recognised the need to provide clean water and proper sewage disposal that diseases such as typhus and cholera disappeared. In 1859 Glasgow was the first city in Scotland to provide a regular supply of clean piped water. When cholera returned to Scotland in 1865 only 53 Glaswegians died of the disease, compared with the 3000 who died in the 1832 epidemic.

Poor health was common among the poor, caused by an inadequate diet (see Source G) and unhealthy working conditions. Those born in 1870 could expect, on average, to live until just 41 years old if male, and just 43 years if female.

Question

1. How useful is Source H as evidence of housing conditions in Scotland at the end of the nineteenth century?

Extension tasks

1. 'In the long run, the Industrial Revolution and its consequences benefited the people of Scotland.'

   Prepare a short speech either agreeing or disagreeing with this statement. Remember that you should use as much evidence as possible in your argument. You should consider both the short-term and the long-term effects of industrialisation.

2. Find out what others in your class think about this issue. You could create a class display to show some of the results of the Industrial Revolution.